MADE AT Y CRËWYD YN Y
SHERMAN 2024

THE WIFE OF CYNCOED

By / Gan Matt Hartley

Cast

Jayne Vivien Parry

AF072745

Creative Team / Tîm Creadigol

Director / Cyfarwyddwr **Hannah Noone**
Designer / Cynllunydd **April Dalton**
Lighting Designer / Cynllunydd Goleuo **Katy Morison**
Composer and Sound Designer / Cyfansoddwr a Chynllunydd Sain **Sam Jones**

Production Team / Tîm Cynhyrchu

Production Manager / Rheolwr Cynhyrchu **Mandy Ivory-Castile**
Company Stage Manager / Rheolwr Llwyfan y Cwmni **Josh Miles**
Deputy Stage Manager / Dirprwy Reolwr Llwyfan **Amy Liddington**
Assistant Stage Manager / Rheolwr Llwyfan Cynorthwyol **Emily Howard**
Technical Manager / Rheolwr Technegol **Rachel Mortimer**
Technicians / Technegwyr **Ruby James, Charlie Moore, Lydia Coomes, Weronika Szumelda**
Workshop Manager / Rheolwr Gweithdy **Alasdair Head**
Construction / Adeiladwaith **Mathew Thomas**
Costume Assistant / Cynorthwyydd Gwisgoedd **Celia Favorite**
RWCMD Student Construction Placement / Lleoliad Myfyriwr Adeiladu CBCDC **Harry Hughes**
Scenic Artist / Artist Golygfaol **Emily Jones**
BSL Interpreter / Dehonglwr BSL **Claire Anderson**
Captioner / Capsiynau **Erika James**
Audio Description / Sain Ddisgrifio **Jana Holesworth**

Sherman Cymru Productions Ltd | Registered Charity Number / Rhif Elusen Cofrestredig 1118364

MAKING THEATRE IS A TEAM EFFORT. IT REQUIRES A BROAD RANGE OF SKILLS AND EXPERTISE TO MAKE A PRODUCTION HAPPEN. THIS IS THE SHERMAN TEAM: / GWAITH TÎM YW CREU THEATR. MAE GOFYN AM YSTOD EANG O SGILIAU AC ARBENIGEDD I GREU CYNHYRCHIAD. DYMA DÎM Y SHERMAN:

Executive / Gweithredol

Artistic Director / Cyfarwyddwr Artistig
Joe Murphy

Chief Executive / Prif Weithredwr
Julia Barry

Artistic Administration / Gweinyddiaeth Artistig

Producing and Programming Manager (Interim)
Rheolwr Cynhyrchu a Rhaglennu (Dros Dro)
Patricia O'Sullivan

Creative Engagement / Ymgysylltu Creadigol

Creative Engagement Manager
Rheolwr Ymgysylltu Creadigol
Francesca Pickard

Creative Engagement Assistant
Cynorthwyydd Ymgysylltu Creadigol
Ffion Denman

Finance and Administration / Cyllid a Gweinyddiaeth

Head of Finance and Administration
Pennaeth Cyllid a Gweinyddiaeth
Sally Shepherd

Company Administrator / Gweinyddwr Cwmni
Helen Macintyre

Finance and Administration Assistant
Cynorthwyydd Cyllid a Gweinyddiaeth
Mikey Porter

Front of House / Blaen y Tŷ

Head of Operations / Pennaeth Gweithrediadau
Kevin Burt

Visitor Experience and Volunteers Manager
Rheolwr Profiad Ymwelwyr a Gwirfoddolwyr
Aled Wyn Thomas

Bar and Kitchen Manager / Rheolwr y Bar a'r Gegin
Anne Marie Saunders

Bar and Kitchen Supervisor / Goruchwyliwr y Bar a'r Gegin
Elicia Axon

Bar and Kitchen Assistants / Cynorthwywyr Bar a Chegin
Nimat Awoyemi, Tom Bently, Tabitha Benton-Evans, Katie Dobbins, Megan Featherstone, Charlotte Limb, Cata Lindegaard, Enfys Macmillan, Maddie Miles, Roisin Miller-O'Brian, Scarlet Morley, Ben Moruzzi, Alexander Prime, Gethin Roberts, Harrison Smith, Elin Stagg, Isabelle Tischler

Fundraising and Development / Codi Arian a Datblygu

Head of Fundraising and Development
Pennaeth Codi Arian a Datblygu
Emma Tropman

Literary / Llenyddol

Literary Manager / Rheolwr Llenyddol
Davina Moss

Literary Associate / Cydymaith Llenyddol
Lowri Morgan

Marketing and Communications / Marchnata a Chyfathrebu

Head of Marketing and Communications
Pennaeth Marchnata a Chyfathrebu
Ed Newsome

Marketing Manager / Rheolwr Marchnata
Alice Smith

Press Manager (Freelance) / Rheolwr y Wasg (Llawrydd)
Catrin Rogers

Marketing Assistant / Cynorthwyydd Marchnata
Carys Evans

Box Office Supervisors / Goruchwylwyr y Swyddfa Docynnau
Scott Frankton, Llion Parry

Box Office Assistants / Cynorthwywyr y Swyddfa Docynnau
Owen Alun, Charla Grace, Johnny Harman, Alice Kilgarriff, Eileen Leahy, Lowri Morgan, Elizabeth Ribchester, Gethin Roberts

***Production and Planning** / Cynhyrchu a Chynllunio*
Head of Production and Planning
Pennaeth Cynhyrchu a Chynllunio
Mandy Ivory-Castile

Company Stage Manager / Rheolwr Llwyfan y Cwmni
Josh Miles

Technical Manager / Rheolwr Technegol
Rachel Mortimer

Workshop Manager / Rheolwr Gweithdy
Alasdair Head

Thank you to our incredible Volunteer Ushers:
Diolch yn fawr i'n Tywyswyr Gwirfoddol anhygoel:
Abbas Radaideh, Ali Robinson, Amy Pilcher, Amy Woods, Anna Lam, Anna Maria Olshansky, Ben Ping, Callum Thomas, Cate Welsh, Charles Gabe, Chloe Parkes, Claire Anderson, Clive Rudge, Clive Ward, Dana Tait, Dave Webb, David Jones, David Prew, Dylan Chichester, Eileen Leahy, Emily Allan, Germaine Walsh, Grace Uruski, Hannah Quinn, Helen Rankmore, India Thomas, Irina Guliaeva, Izzy Brain, Jack Brown, Jack Stokes, Jaya Dodiya, Jenny Cripps, Jen Sutton, Kalila Bradley, Kate McCann, Katie Brown, Kevin Chubb, Lizzie Moreland, Lucia Taher, Lucinda Devine, Madalena Juma, Magdalena Sowka, Martin Gray, Mary Prew, Mary Rudge, Mehdi Razi, Nick Fisk, Paige Cooper, Paul Mitchell, Peter Gaskell, Radu Harnu, Rhys Evans, Rubie Fallon, Sian Davies, Sue Hayes, Taskin Ar-Rafee, Terri Delahunty, Theo Greenwood, Tom Rhys, Tony Wu

BOARD OF TRUSTEES / YMDDIRIEDOLWYR
Ceri Davies *(Chair / Cadeirydd)*
Rhian Head *(Vice Chair / Is-gadeirydd)*
Nicholas Carlton
Llinos Daniel
Alex Hicks
Ifty Khan
David King MBE
Márta Minier
Gary Owen
Marc Simcox
Huw Thomas
Louise Thomas
Owen Thomas
Jane Tyler
Helen Vallis

WELCOME / CROESO

Whether you are joining us in person or are reading at home, welcome to *The Wife of Cyncoed* – our first Made at Sherman production of 2024. We are once again sharing a Cardiff story with universal reach, written by a brilliant local writer in a production made under our roof in Cathays. Through Matt's beautiful new play, Hannah and Vivien invite us to see the world through the eyes of a woman in her 60s. Older people, particularly older women, can be invisible in our society and this isn't the kind of story we often get to hear. *The Wife of Cyncoed* is a howl of rage against how older women are overlooked and are written out of the narrative. In this hugely funny new play, women like Jayne are at the heart of the story.

P'un a ydych yn ymuno â ni yn y theatr neu'n darllen adref, croeso i *The Wife of Cyncoed* – ein cynhyrchiad Crëwyd yn y Sherman cyntaf yn 2024. Unwaith eto, rhannwn stori o Gaerdydd sydd â chyrhaeddiad rhyngwladol, wedi'i hysgrifennu gan ysgrifennwr arbennig sy'n lleol i'r ardal ac wedi'i chynhyrchu o dan ein to yn Cathays. Trwy ddrama newydd a hyfryd Matt, cawn ein gwahodd gan Hannah a Vivien i weld y byd trwy lygaid dynes yn ei 60au. Gall pobl hŷn, yn enwedig menywod hŷn, fod yn anweledig o fewn ein cymdeithas a ni chawn glywed stori fel hon yn aml. Mae *The Wife of Cyncoed* yn floedd ffyrnig yn erbyn sut caiff menywod hŷn eu hanwybyddu a'u hysgrifennu o'r naratif. Yn y ddrama newydd a digri hon, mae menywod fel Jayne wrth galon y stori.

Joe Murphy
Artistic Director / Cyfarwyddwr Artistig

Julia Barry
Chief Executive / Prif Weithredwr

CARDIFF'S THEATRE FOR WALES

Imagine a world made more equitable, more compassionate, more unified by the power of theatre. We are driven to achieve this vision every day. We do this by creating and curating shared live theatre experiences that inspire people from all backgrounds across South Wales to make a better world, in their own way. We believe that access to creativity and self-expression is a right and we constantly strive to ensure everyone has the opportunity to be enriched by the art of theatre.

THEATR I GYMRU YNG NGHAERDYDD

Dychmygwch fyd lle gall pŵer y theatr greu byd tecach, mwy tosturiol ac unedig. Cawn ein hysgogi i gyflawni'r weledigaeth yma yn ddyddiol. Rydyn ni'n gwneud hyn drwy greu a churadu profiadau theatr byw i'w rhannu ac i ysbrydoli pobl o bob cefndir ar draws De Cymru i fedru gwneud byd gwell, yn eu ffordd eu hunain. Credwn fod pawb â'r hawl i gael mynediad at greadigrwydd a hunanfynegiant, ac ymdrechwn yn gyson i sicrhau bod pawb yn cael y cyfle i gael eu cyfoethogi gan y theatr.

SHERMANTHEATRE.CO.UK

CAST

VIVIEN PARRY
Jayne

Theatre includes / Theatr yn cynnwys: *Cabaret* (West End); *Sydney and the Old Girl* (Park Theatre); *Les Misérables* (Queen's Theatre); *A Christmas Carol, Twelfth Night, A Midsummer Night's Dream, The Shoemaker's Holiday* (RSC); *The Girls* (UK tour / taith DU); *Half a Sixpence* (Noël Coward Theatre); *Top Hat* (Aldwych Theatre); *Blackthorn, Shakespeare's Will, Great Expectations, Macbeth, Arcadia, The Crucible, Betrayal, Bedroom Farce, Abigail's Party, The Norman Conquests* (Theatr Clwyd); *Memory* (The Pleasance/59E59 Broadway); *The Swing of Things* (Stephen Joseph Theatre); *Mamma Mia!* (Prince of Wales Theatre); *The Resistible Rise of Arturo Ui* (Citizens Theatre); *Boston Marriage* (Octagon Theatre); *The Ash Girl* (Birmingham Rep); *Sadly Solo Jo* (Greenwich); *Fame* (Cambridge Theatre); *Which Witch* (Piccadilly Theatre); *Blood Brothers* (Phoenix Theatre).

Film and television includes / Ffilm a theledu yn cynnwys:
Disney's Beauty and the Beast, Holby City, Crash, Outside the Rules, The Bench, The Bill, Nuts and Bolts, The Comedy Show, Llafur Cariad, Dirty Work, Victorian Diary.

Radio includes / Radio yn cynnwys: *Monster, The Berlin Diaries, Touching the Linden Tree, The Tales of Lady Murasaki, The Starving Girl of Llanfihangel.*

CREATIVE TEAM / TÎM CREADIGOL

MATT HARTLEY
Writer / Ysgrifennwr

Matt Hartley studied Drama at the University of Hull and lives in Cardiff with his family. His first play *Sixty-Five Miles* won a Bruntwood Award and was produced by Paines Plough / Hull Truck Theatre. Since then he has forged a career writing for theatre, television and radio.

Matt's theatre work has been produced at venues and companies including; Shakespeare's Globe (*Eyam*), Royal Shakespeare Company

(*Myth* co-written with Kirsty Housley), Pentabus Theatre (*Here I Belong / Idyll*), Hampstead Theatre (*Deposit*), Soho Theatre (*Microcosm*), National Theatre (*Horizon* NT Connections), and is regularly produced and revived internationally. Matt's play *Girl* is the winner of the Prix Godot and will receive its World Premiere in spring 2024 at NCAD Dunkerque in France.

Radio 4 work includes: *The Pursuit, Tracks, Final Call, Release, Bad Ark*.

For television Matt has written on returning shows such as *Hollyoaks* and *EastEnders*. Currently Matt has his own original projects in development with multiple production companies and broadcasters including the BBC, ITV, Channel 4 and Netflix.

Astudiodd Matt Hartley Drama ym Mhrifysgol Hull a nawr mae'n byw yng Nghaerdydd gyda'i deulu. Enillodd ei ddrama gyntaf *Sixty-Five Miles* Wobr Bruntwood a gafodd ei gynhyrchu gan Paines Plough / Hull Truck Theatre. Ers hynny mae wedi creu gyrfa lwyddiannus yn ysgrifennu ar gyfer theatr, teledu a radio.

Mae gwaith theatr Matt wedi'i gynhyrchu gan sawl cwmni ar draws y wlad gan gynnwys; Shakespeare's Globe (*Eyam*), Royal Shakespeare Company (*Myth*, a gafodd ei gyd-ysgrifennu gyda Kirsty Housely), Pentabus Theatre (*Here i Belong / Idyll*), Hampstead Theatre (*Deposit*), Soho Theatre (*Microcosm*), National Theatre (*Horizon* NT Connections), ac yn cael ei gynhyrchu'n rheolaidd a'i adfywio'n rhyngwladol. Fydd drama Matt, *Girl*, enillydd o'r Prix Godot, yn cael ei ddangosiad rhyngwladol cyntaf yng ngwanwyn 2024 yn NCAD Dunkerque yn Ffrainc.

Mae ei waith ar gyfer Radio 4 yn cynnwys: *The Pursuit, Tracks, Final Call, Release, Bad Ark*.

Ar gyfer teledu, mae Matt wedi ysgrifennu ar gyfer sawl sioe gan gynnwys *Hollyoaks* ac *EastEnders*. Ar hyn o bryd mae Matt yn datblygu ei brosiectau gwreiddiol ei hun gyda nifer o gwmnïau cynhyrchu a darlledwyr gan gynnwys y BBC, ITV, Channel 4 a Netflix.

HANNAH NOONE
Director / Cyfarwyddwr

Hannah is a UK based theatre & opera director from North Wales who has worked on multi award-winning plays, operas and musicals, including the first UK National Tour of Olivier Award winning *Home, I'm Darling*, alongside co-director Tamara Harvey.

Mae Hannah yn gyfarwyddwr theatr ac opera yn y DU sy'n dod o Ogledd Cymru ac wedi gweithio ar ddramâu, operâu a sioeau cerdd arobryn, gan gynnwys taith gyntaf y DU o ddrama sydd wedi ennill un o Wobrau Olivier, *Home, I'm Darling*, ochr yn ochr â'i chyd-gyfarwyddwr Tamara Harvey.

For Sherman Theatre / Ar gyfer Theatr y Sherman: *Deg / Ten, Between Eternity and Time* (co-production with RWCMD / cyd-gynhyrchiad gyda CBCDC).

Theatre includes / Theatr yn cynnwys: *Cinderella, The Snow Queen* (Storyhouse); *Truth* (Theatr Clwyd); Co-Director with Tamara Harvey for UK Tour of / Cyd-Gyfarwyddwr gyda Tamara Harvey ar gyfer Taith DU o *Home, I'm Darling* (National Theatre / Theatr Clwyd / Bill Kenwright); *The Welkin* (RWCMD at Sherman Theatre / CBCDC yn Theatr y Sherman); *The In-Between* (National Youth Theatre of Wales / Theatr Cenedlaethol Ieuenctid Cymru / Theatr Clwyd); *London Road, Wife, Arcadia* (RWCMD / CBCDC); *A Building Made of Stories* (Theatr Clwyd); *Nightmare Scenario* (Opera Sonic); *Worlds Apart in War* (Theatr Clwyd / National Trust); Offie-nominated / wedi'i enwebu am Offie *The Elixir of Love* (King's Head Theatre); *BoHo* (Theatr Clwyd / Hijinx).

Associate directing includes / Cyfarwyddo cyswllt yn cynnwys: *Double Drop* (Dirty Protest / Edinburgh Fringe); *Home, I'm Darling* (West End transfer / trosglwyddiad West End / National Theatre / Theatr Clwyd); *Uncle Vanya* (Sheffield Theatres / Theatr Clwyd).

Assistant directing includes / Cyfarwyddo cynorthwyol yn cynnwys: *Wolf, Witch, Giant, Fairy* (Royal Opera House); *A New Dark Age* (Royal Opera House); *Mr Gum & the Dancing Bear* (National Theatre); *The Assassination of Katie Hopkins* (Theatr Clwyd); *La Bohème* (OperaUpClose).

APRIL DALTON
Designer / Cynllunydd

April Dalton is a UK based Set and Costume Designer for Theatre, Opera and Dance. April is Co-Artistic Director of Red Oak Theatre, Sherman Theatre's Company in Residence. She graduated from the Royal Welsh College of Music and Drama in Theatre Design, winning the Costume Design Award. After graduating, April's work was shortlisted for the Linbury Prize for Stage Design.

Mae April Dalton yn Gynllunydd Set a Gwisgoedd ar gyfer Theatr, Opera a Dawns yn y DU. Mae April yn Gyd-gyfarwyddwr Artistig gyda Red Oak Theatre, Cwmni Preswyl Theatr y Sherman. Graddiodd o Goleg Brenhinol Cerdd a Drama Cymru yn Cynllunio Theatr, gan ennill y Wobr Cynllunio Gwisgoedd. Ar ôl graddio, roedd gwaith April ar y rhestr fer am Wobr Linbury ar gyfer Cynllunio Llwyfan.

Design highlights include / Uchafbwyntiau cynllunio yn cynnwys: *The Odyssey: The Lotus Eaters* (Restoke / National Theatre); *Baroque Encounters, Solace, Remembrance, Four Seasons* (New English Ballet Theatre, The Linbury Theatre, Royal Opera House); *Silla* (Northern

Opera Group); *The Return of Ulysses, La Liberazione di Ruggiero, Spell Book* (Longborough Festival Opera); *Migrations, Le Vin Herbe, FREEDOM Season* (Welsh National Opera / Opera Cenedlaethol Cymru); *Imminent* (Birmingham Royal Ballet); *Cherubin, Triple Bill* including the world premiere of *WITCH* / yn cynnwys y dangosiad rhyngwladol cyntaf o *WITCH* (Royal Academy of Music); *Der Zaubertrank* (Theater und Konzert St. Gallen); *Dido and Aeneas, La Belle Helene* (Blackheath Halls Opera).

KATY MORISON
Lighting Designer / Cynllunydd Goleuo

Katy is an experienced Lighting Designer working throughout the UK. She is highly respected by directors, working across a variety of productions.

She is a lecturer and supervisor at the Royal Welsh College of Music and Drama and was part of the lighting team at Sherman Theatre for many years. Katy has worked as an Associate Designer and re-lighter for major productions and renowned lighting designers.

Mae Katy yn Gynllunydd Goleuo profiadol sy'n gweithio ledled y DU. Mae'n uchel ei pharch gyda chyfarwyddwyr, yn gweithio ar draws amrywiaeth o gynyrchiadau.

Mae'n ddarlithydd ac yn oruchwyliwr yng Ngholeg Brenhinol Cerdd a Drama Cymru a bu'n rhan o dîm goleuo Theatr y Sherman am flynyddoedd lawer. Mae Katy wedi gweithio fel Cydymaith Cynllunio ac fel ail-oleuwr ar gyfer cynyrchiadau mawreddog a chynllunwyr goleuo adnabyddus.

For Sherman Theatre / Ar gyfer Theatr y Sherman:
Elen Benfelen / Goldilocks, A Hero of the People, The Snow Queen, Woof, Alice in Wonderland, Little Red Riding Hood / Yr Hugan Fach Goch, Corina Pavlova and the Lion's Roar / Corina Pavlova a'r Llew Sy'n Rhuo, The Snow Tiger / Teigr yr Eira.

Theatre includes / Theatr yn cynnwys: *Cinderella* (Storyhouse, Chester / Caer); *The Suspicions of Mr Whicher* (Watermill); *Waldo's Circus of Magic & Terror* (Bristol Old Vic / UK tour / taith DU / Extraordinary Bodies); *A Gig for Ghosts* (Soho Upstairs / 45North); *A Dead Body in Taos, The Litten Trees* (Fuel Theatre); *The In-Between* (National Youth Arts Wales / Celfyddydau Cenedlaethol Ieuenctid Cymru and / a Theatr Clwyd); *Anthem* (Wales Millennium Centre / Canolfan Mileniwm Cymru); *A Tale of Two Cities* (Lost Dog Dance); *Anfamol* (Theatr Genedlaethol Cymru); *Typical Girls* (Clean Break / Sheffield Theatres); *Possible, Peggy's Song, For All I Care, Come Back Tomorrow, The Big Democracy Project* (National Theatre Wales); *Why Are People Clapping; Moving Is Everywhere, Forever* (National Dance Company Wales / Cwmni Dawns Cenedlaethol Cymru); *The Glee Club* (Stockroom);

American Nightmare, The Story, Hela, Seanmhair, Play / Silence, Sand, St Nicholas, Constellation Street, A Good Clean Heart (The Other Room); Exodus, The Good Earth (Motherlode); Crouch, Touch, Pause, Engage (National Theatre Wales and / a Out of Joint); Escape the Scaffold (The Other Room and / a Theatre 503); Sinners Club (The Other Room, Gagglebabble and / a Theatr Clwyd).

SAM JONES
Composer and Sound Designer
Cyfansoddwr a Chynllunydd Sain

Sam is a composer, music producer, sound designer and engineer. He works across projects in theatre, screen and music.

Mae Sam yn gyfansoddwr, cynhyrchydd cerdd, cynllunydd a pheiriannydd sain. Mae'n gweithio ar draws prosiectau mewn theatr, sgrin a cherdd.

For Sherman Theatre / Ar gyfer Theatr y Sherman: *Imrie* (co-production with / cyd-gynhyrchiad gyda Frân Wen); *Iphigenia in Splott*; *Tylwyth* (co-production with / cyd-gynhyrchiad gyda Theatr Genedlaethol Cymru); *Lose Yourself*; *Woof*; *Tremor*, *The Mother****er With The Hat* (co-production with / cyd-gynhyrchiad gyda Tron Theatre); *Love, Cardiff: City Road Stories*; *Home/Cartref*; *The Weir* (co-production with / cyd-gynhyrchiad gyda Tobacco Factory Theatres).

Recent work includes / Gwaith diweddar yn cynnwys: *Cinderella* (Storyhouse Live Chester / Caer); *Popeth ar y Ddaear*, *Anweledig* (Frân Wen); *FRANK* (Jones Collective/National Theatre Wales); *Possible, For All I Care* (National Theatre Wales); *Faust+Greta* (Frân Wen / Theatr Genedlaethol Cymru); *The World's Wife* (Welsh National Opera / Opera Cenedlaethol Cymru); *Saethu Cwningod / Shooting Rabbits* (PowderHouse in association with Sherman Theatre and Theatr Genedlaethol Cymru / mewn cysylltiad gyda Theatr y Sherman a Theatr Genedlaethol Cymru); *The Sinners Club* (Gagglebabble / The Other Room / Theatr Clwyd); *Y Ferch gyda'r Gwallt Hynod Hir / The Girl with Incredibly Long Hair* (We Made This); *The Last Five Years* (Leeway Productions / Wales Millenium Centre / Canolfan Mileniwm Cymru); *Tuck* (Neontopia / Wales Millenium Centre / Canolfan Mileniwm Cymru); *St Nicholas, Sand* (The Other Room); *Looking Through Glass* (difficult|stage); *This Incredible Life* (Canoe Theatre).

SHERMAN +

Get closer to exceptional theatre today with a Sherman+ Membership.

Dewch yn nes at theatr eithriadol heddiw gydag Aelodaeth Sherman+.

Sherman+ members get access to special events and content, offering unique insights into how theatre is made from the people who make it.

JOIN TODAY AND RECEIVE:

- Invitations to exclusive events at Sherman Theatre, led by artists and theatre makers.
- An invitation to an annual supporters' event hosted by our Artistic Director and members of the Sherman team.
- A Behind the Scenes tour for all new members.
- Member newsletter.
- A dedicated ticket booking service through a direct line to our Fundraising department.
- An acknowledgement of your support on the Sherman Theatre website.

Sherman+ membership costs £20 per month. Minimum 12 months term.

Mae aelodau Sherman+ yn cael mynediad i ddigwyddiadau a chynnwys arbennig sy'n cynnig cipolwg unigryw gan grewyr theatr ar sut maen nhw'n mynd ati i greu eu gwaith.

YMUNWCH HEDDIW I GAEL:

- Gwahoddiad i ddigwyddiadau ecsgliwsif yn Theatr y Sherman o dan arweiniad artistiaid a chrewyr theatr.
- Gwahoddiad i'n digwyddiad blynyddol i gefnogwyr a gynhelir gan ein Cyfarwyddwr Artistig ac aelodau o dîm y Sherman.
- Taith Tu ôl i'r Llen i bob aelod newydd.
- Cylchlythyr aelodau.
- Gwasanaeth archebu tocynnau ymroddedig drwy linell uniongyrchol i'n hadran Codi Arian.
- Cydnabyddiaeth o'ch cefnogaeth ar wefan Theatr y Sherman.

Mae aelodaeth Sherman+ yn costio £20 y mis. Isafswm o 12 mis.

JOIN TODAY:
YMUNWCH HEDDIW:

THE WIFE OF CYNCOED

Acknowledgements

Deep thanks to all those who have helped bring this to life. Rachel O'Riordan for getting the ball rolling. Giles Smart, David Mercatali, Branwen Davies, Caroline Berry, Julia Barry and the entire staff at the Sherman for all the work they have given to help shape and bring this show to life.

Davina Moss for diving into the guts and Joe Murphy for all his wit, wisdom and continual belief in the project. The fantastic creative team: Amy, Emily, Josh, April, Katy and Sam. Huge thanks to the wonderful Hannah Noone and Vivien Parry for being so bold, playful and reminding me why I started writing plays in the first place.

My daughter and all her grandparents for their inspiration (and free childcare).

And my wife who loves love.

M.H.

Character

JAYNE, *sixty-six*

Notes on the Text

A dash (–) at the end of a line indicates an interrupted thought or unfinished sentence.

An ellipsis (…) suggests a loaded or pregnant pause.

A dash (–) alone on a line indicates a new moment in time.

An ellipsis (…) alone on a line indicates a thought, silence or inarticulation.

Notes on Location

Cyncoed is an affluent suburb in Cardiff. It's historically aspirational and where people with money in the city often live or want to live. Anyone from Cardiff would understand what that name represents. Any location change would need to reflect that. For example, if it was set in Sheffield it would be The Wife of Dore; in Bristol – The Wife of Clifton; Manchester – The Wife of Hale, etc.

This text went to press before the end of rehearsals and so may differ slightly from the play as performed.

Penny's holding court.

She's there, she is, swinging gently back, forth, in the egg chair I's had my eye on all afternoon.

And I'm trying not to listen in, I'm just trying to enjoy my little glass of Prosecco but there is a lot of laughter coming from all those listening to her story.

Portugal – that is the word that I can't help but focus on.

Penny's saying about why they chose to get a villa there:

That it's better than Spain, that you gets more for your money.

But mostly how it is for Malcolm, my ex, her husband, and his golfing.

'Not that the courses are thanking us,' Penny says, 'every time he plays a round, he digs a new bunker.'

And Malcolm, do you know what he's doing, he's stood there smiling, he's actually got his hands up, playfully protesting, as Penny makes this joke at his expense.

'Are you alright there?'

It takes me a moment to realise Penny's talking to me. Somehow, see, I've just ended up in the midst of this group.

'Oh, sorry, ignore me', and I looks at Dave, my son-in law, and goes, 'I's just admiring the egg chair. New isn't it.'

Dave just nods, sips his beer.

'John Lewis, right, Dave?'

'Better ask your daughter. I just pay for it.'

I'm suddenly telling everyone that I've got my eye on one too. That I got a few vouchers from work on my last day. Put them towards it. How I's got a real sun trap down the back of my garden.

Mixture of nods and smiles, sips of drinks, greet me back. Then Dave goes he is off to get another beer and asks if anyone else wants one. And a few others, say 'I'll come too' and starts to head back towards the house with him.

'Would you like to give it a try?'

Penny's asking as she gracefully hops out.

'No, no, don't get out on my account.'

'Honestly, it's fine, I think we've all had enough out here anyway.'

I look up at Penny, her hair glistening in the sun and try to match her smile.

'Will you be alright getting in?'

Malcolm actually seems concerned as he asks. As if he's dealing with someone really old, like the way he used to speak to his mother in her last few years.

Penny slaps him on the arm.

'She'll be plenty fine.'

I watch them walk back up towards the house. Malcolm's hand it's resting on Penny's bum, guiding her to where all the noise is now spilling out from.

I feel the sun on me.

I push the egg swing a little. Test it. Springier than I thought.

I goes to get in –

'Mam, there you are.'

It's Emma, she's come walking over with Jacob, my grandson, in her arms.

'I could really do with your help, you know.'

The smell hits me, a one-year-old's diet: Breast milk, mixed with mashed sweet potato, and broccoli – however used to it, it can't help but make your eyes water.

'Come here, Nanny will take care of you.'

It is not the easiest nappy change. It's one of those ones, you know, where it's all leaked out of the side. I tries to distract myself a little from the smell and the flecks of broccoli trapped under his scrotum by looking at the photos they got all framed up around his nursery.

Jacob there in Emma's arms just after he has been born. All sweat and tears and love.

Clara, my eldest grandchild, probably, what just turned two, with me pushing her in the swings down by the lake.

Next to that there's a photo of Malcolm, Penny, Emma, Jacob and Clara all smiles as they sit together eating lunch at the villa in Portugal, by the side of its sparkling pool.

It gets me thinking about my passport, about where I put it.

Truth be told, I don't even know if it is in date any more.

As I spread a bit of Sudocrem on Jacob's bum, I can hear Emma chatting downstairs:

'Dad, your glass is empty, let me get you a drink.'

'Oh, go on, you twisted my arm. Tell Penny I's just going to spend one.'

I go to shut Jacob's door, but –

Malcolm's there. He takes a really long moment to consider us –

'He's a healthy young man, that's for sure.'

The bathroom door closes behind him.

The rest of the party flies by really.

I watch Emma and Dave wave people goodbyes from the window as I load the dishes. I close the dishwasher up. Look round for what to do next.

'Mam, me and Dave have had some drinks, and we've got to start getting them to bed soon, will you be alright getting a taxi?'

'Put it on my account,' Dave adds as he swigs another beer. I tell them he doesn't need to do that. He nods and heads back through to the lounge. Golf starts on the TV seconds later.

Clara and Jacob they give me so many kisses when the taxi pulls up. Emma has to almost prise them back off my legs, 'Relax', she tells them, 'you'll see Nanny on Thursday. *Nanny Daycare*.'

Malcolm and Penny are stood by their new *Jaguar*.

'We'd offer a lift but it's basically a two-seater.'

'It's fine, it's fine.'

And Penny gives me the biggest smile as she says it was so lovely to see me.

'Nice house.' The taxi driver says as he pulls out onto Lisvane Road.

'My daughter and her husband's.'

'*He* must have good job.'

I nod. I guess Dave has. Same could be said for Emma too though.

—

Back before the divorce, when we lived in Cyncoed, on Dan-y-Coed Road, Emma used to always give me a row about cleaning: 'God, Mam, not the vacuum again, it's like it's your best friend!'

'You'll understand one day', I'd tell her, 'when you have a family, a husband, how important it is to keep a tidy house.'

'I'll just get a cleaner, like Hannah's mum.'

After Malcom walked out, not long after he made me sell the house, and this here, is what his financial settlement stretched to in the Cardiff High catchment area.

'A wonderfully homely, two-bed maisonette, with panoramic views of the lake' according to the estate agent.

Those first few months in here, I let things slip a bit. Dust would settle. Surfaces got sticky.

And oh god the screaming rows were even bigger with me and Emma.

'I'm not sharing a room with Andrew, I want to go and stay with Dad.'

And I'd tell her: Yeah that's fine, please do, bet your father's new girlfriend would love to spend all her time washing your dirty underwear.

Emma never did, and I bought a sofa bed, so they each had their own room, and I started properly cleaning again, because you know what I realised: that even if I was no longer in my dream home I was still house proud.

So that's what I do when I gets back in. I gives the surfaces a good clean, carpets a nice vacuum, then finally I tops up the water for the flowers I got from work. The card that they all signed is up next to it on the mantelpiece.

'LIFE BEGINS NOW' in big letters it says.

Read some of the messages:

'Jealous! Paul.'

'It was nice working with you. Best, Andrea.' Thirteen years we sat opposite each other.

I puts the card back and –

I catch sight of my nan in the mirror.

Not possible, she has been dead going on forty years.

…

My mam would always say how I looked like her mother. She meant it as a compliment, as apparently, in her prime, Nan was a real looker.

I only knew her as an old lady though.

Shrunken.

The bin bag's full by the time I've finished. Barely a walk to where the wheelie is but I still put my coat on and head out. I lifts the bin lid up and –

There's not enough space for my bag, which, as I've only put one bag in since they last collected it, should make no sense, but it does.

Gill, two doors up at number eight. See, she's been dumping her excess rubbish in my wheelie bin. What she does is, she lifts my rubbish what I's already put in, then puts hers under so she doesn't think I'd notice.

But I do.

And I know she doesn't do it with Brian and Tiffany who lives next door, at six, she does it just with me…

I look at Gill's house, feel the weight of the bin bag in my hand.

…

Bins get collected on Wednesday, I says to myself. Not long.

–

It's the sound of birds that wakes me up.

What do I do now with this time I have for myself?

A leisurely rise, then treat myself by heading down to Café Terra Nova on Roath Park Lake.

Sits there with my cappuccino watching the swans teaching their cygnets how to swim.

Have a wander through the rose garden after.

Look at all the daffodils coming out.

That's what I'll do.

Nothing major.

Just like I said to everyone when they asked how I was going to spend my retirement:

'Oh nothing grand. Bit of telly, sorting out the loft, bit of peace.'

(JAYNE *snorts like her sister.*)

'You shoulds get a dog. Do you wonders. The *company*. The *exercise*.'

My sister, when I said that was my plan:

'What you implying?'

'You know. Days are long when you got no one to share them with.'

'No, no, I'll be fine.'

'I suppose you got the practice.'

There she was, nearly twenty years on still savouring any moment to remind me that Malcolm walked out on me.

'Oh, here she is, the Wife of Cyncoed' she used to say to our mam when I'd go to visit them down the house that we all grew up in Rhymney. 'Back slumming it with us commoners.'

And Mam would nod.

The shower's lovely and hot.

I can hear my mobile ringing.

I let it ring out.

But now the house phone's going, and it doesn't stop, just keeps ringing and ringing.

'I been calling and calling.'

Emma's voice is going a million miles an hour.

'I was in the shower.'

'I've got an emergency in work, I have to go in, I need your help with the kids.'

As she keeps talking I zone out, like I'm having déjà vu, like those exact words have been said before.

Almost two and half years ago, when I went to three days a week and Emma first asked me to look after Clara for one, then not long after two days a week, whilst she went back to work.

I said to her then 'what about your father, you asked him, could he do a day'?

Oh, Emma she thought that was hilarious.

'They only live in Ogmore. He's retired, isn't he? So he's got plenty of time, might just have do a round less of golf a week.'

'Mam, don't you want to help look after your grandchild? It's a real treat to have that time with her.'

…

I'm just dressed by the time they pull up outside.

Emma's heartbeat is pounding out of her chest as she tells me: 'They've had a snack but could do with a proper breakfast.'

'Maybe you should just say you can't come in today, lovely.'

'Mam, *you* have no idea.'

–

Come rain or shine, Thursdays and Fridays I takes them down the playground by Roath Lake.

I always tell Clara: Swans always need feeding. Squirrels chasing and swings playing on.

So today won't be any different.

Busy already when we get down, but funny thing is I don't recognise anyone. If it had been Thursday or Friday, I'd be sure I'd recognise at least ten or so people. All of us in our similar routines.

Most of them are younger mums, a few dads too – fair play, modern – little packs of groups over time they've formed.

And they are perfectly nice to me, but you know I don't go to the café after or –

We nod hellos basically.

So it is weird being there on a different day, a stranger in a new land.

I put Jacob in the swing and give him a push whilst Clara plays on the pirate ship.

THE WIFE OF CYNCOED

Try to focus on the wind brushing through the trees not the shrieking and screaming from all around.

'Grandad!'

'Yes, Elsie?'

'Higher!!'

I look over to the swing next to me.

My throat seizes up.

My neck starts to itch.

My palms sweat.

I don't have a type.

The men I've known, intimately, and it's not an exhaustive list.

Three.

There's nothing that connects them, physically, or well anything really.

And truth is I never lusted after any of them. Don't get me wrong, over the years I seen men before and I have felt waves of it.

Lust.

So, I know that feeling could exist in me. But it was never about a specific type, it was a feeling I got from them.

And this man, next to me, he has it.

God, he has it.

As he pushes the swing with this little girl in, it's hypnotic.

The gentleness as he laughs with her.

But then this strength.

He's got a polo shirt on. Dark blue. *John Lewis*, home brand.

Oh my, the breadth of him.

Suddenly makes sense why I worked in the hospital for so long, why I sat under pictures of the human anatomy day in day out, it is so that I know exactly what the muscle is called:

The deltoid.

...

The swing hits me on the hip.

I don't know how long I've been staring...

Could be seconds, minutes...

He hasn't seen me though.

Suddenly a child runs in front of the swings. Misses Jacob by millimetres, but his legs aren't fully in time with his body and he trips with a thud straight onto the floor. Every head turns, expecting tears but he just picks himself up and races on towards the slide:

'They bounce don't they.'

It's him.

Deltoids.

Deepest, kindest, brown eyes meeting mine.

And I just nod, then looks back down at Jacob in his swing. My arms they somehow find a way to give it another push.

'Come on then you, let's get you home.'

And he is there lifting the little girl up and out of the swing.

Deltoids pulsing.

I watch them skip away together, all laughter as they head up the slope towards the promenade by the lake.

'Nanny, can I get an ice cream?'

Clara's pulling at my sleeve. Not even eleven but I look up at where the van is, up by the promenade.

'Quickly, then.'

I'm dragging Clara up the slope whilst pushing Jacob in his buggy. Breaths catching as I scan along the promenade.

Buggies, dogs, people milling.

But no Deltoids.

Gone.

—

Twenty past six Emma arrives.

'Clara, this is not funny!'

Which makes Clara wiggle even more as Emma tries to clip her into her car seat.

'Don't fight me.'

'Ow, pinched my leg!!!'

'I said to stop fighting me!'

Emma's rushing back round to the driver's seat, telling me 'I've got so much more work to do when I get home.'

I step back in to the quiet. Allow the peace to seep into me.

My hand is on my shoulder. I don't remember how, it just seems to have drifted there automatically, tracing, feeling the shape of it, of my –

My deltoid.

I'm feeling my deltoid.

Room feels hot.

Radiator's not on.

It's me.

I'm hot and –

The house phone rings.

'Letting me go to voicemail, then, are you, Mother?'

'Oh, hi Andrew. Is it seven thirty already?'

I can imagine him, my boy, looking out of his flat's huge window, still dressed all smart, the hustle of London way down below him.

He starts saying how my first day of retirement must be going well if I'm already losing track of our Monday routine.

'I've had the kids round, must have been having a little daydream now I got my peace back.'

He goes quiet.

'Emma had to go into work at the last minute.'

'Oh yes, the world marches to her beat, I forgot.'

'Andrew –'

'I was just thinking how it's nice that you've set your stall out, that's all.'

It goes quiet again.

'You've been swimming after work then?'

'You know on Monday it's what I do.'

I can hear something in the background. Pans moving, clanking.

'Are you making your pasta tea then, is it, Andrew? Pasta, is it? Andrew?'

'Right. Mother. You're coming to stay with me next Saturday for the weekend.'

'What?'

'We're not having this being how your retirement begins. I'm booking you a train.'

'...Andrew.'

'I won't take no for an answer.'

After we say goodnight, I put the phone down on the table.

Quick vacuum, then head up to bed.

–

I make a trip to Aldi.

Catch up on my *Silent Witnesses*.

Makes a start on the loft... where does all this stuff come from?

Wednesday, I got my hair appointment.

Turns up at five to eleven for my eleven o'clock appointment.
I can see my stylist, Hayley, is still chattering away.
Receptionist pops over.

'You don't mind coming back at twelve as Hayley needs to cram someone in.'

'...of course, sorry, sure.'

I walk up and down Wellfield Road for an hour.

'I won't keep you long, just a trim,' I tell Hayley when she sits me down.

The woman in the chair next to me, she hears my voice and she turns to face me.

'Excuse me,' she goes, 'Do you work down the Heath?'

I'd know this woman's face. Late forties. A real head-turner. And yet I can't place her.

'Oh, apologies I didn't mean to intrude.'

'No, no, sorry, I'm trying to place you.'

'We've never met. I thought I recognised your voice, from, sorry, enjoy your hair cut.'

And she's about to turn back in her chair.

'I do – did work there, I just retired actually.'

'That's a shame. Not for you. I mean for the patients.'

'Oh, I doubt that, I wasn't a doctor or a nurse.'

'You'd be surprised. You don't recognise my voice at all, do you? You were Dr Flooks's secretary.'

'That's right.'

'My husband, Thomas, he was one of his patients.'

'Oh.'

And now I can't help but smile softly. Aware what she means.

'I never actually said thank you, for being so kind, when I would call and arrange his chemo.'

'There was never a need to say that.'

'You had such a calm and kind presence. I couldn't really articulate that then, but I can say that now, so yes, thank you.'

I take her hand, and just hold it as she finishes getting her hair blow dried.

–

It's Monday and Emma's had to go back into work *again*, so I'm back down the park with them.

Clara is being a monster demanding this, demanding that.

'Want to go back, Nanny.'

'We've just got here!'

'Clara!!!!'

It's a little girl I don't know running towards her. Turns out they go to nursery together. And this gives Clara a second wind.

'I don't want to go!!'

'Good, because we're not!'

The two girls run off to the pirate ship.

I push Jacob in his swing. Close my eyes, let the sound of all the shrieking children wash away.

Finally.

Calm.

'Is it hot there?'

He's looking directly at me, he is, pushing the other swing.

Deltoids.

'Sand between my toes, that's what I always picture.'

I can't get any words out.

'Sorry, that's rude of me, ruining your peace.'

And he pushes the swing, looks out over the rest of the playground.

'Sky was bright blue. Not a cloud in the sky,' this time I'm looking at him.

He nods, approving: a good choice.

We keep pushing the swings.

'She yours?' I ask him, pointing at the little girl in the swing.

'Oh no, I get to hand her back at the end of day.'

'I meant –'

And he smiles, clearly he knew exactly what I meant.

'Elsie. My granddaughter. My little girl's girl. You?'

He's looking towards Jacob.

'He's my IVF miracle.'

I hold it for a long time.

'…Congratulations…'

And I give him a nice nod, thanking him. Smirk growing. And he catches me.

'Pulling my leg, aren't you.'

We're both properly smiling now.

'My grandson. Jacob. His sister, Clara, is over there too.'

'I need a poo, Nanny. It's poking out.'

It's Clara waddling back over.

I lift Jacob out of the swing.

'Delightful' I mouth to Deltoids.

'I'm Alun by the way.'

'Alun.'

And he's waiting, he is, waiting for me to do the same.

And so I tell him my name:

'Jayne. I'm Jayne.'

'Be here next week, Jayne?'

'Yeah. Yeah.'

–

Somehow, I'm just suddenly stood in my bedroom alone.

I meet my own reflection in the mirror.

There's a smile looking back at me.

I lie back onto the bed.

I close my eyes.

I imagine the weight of the deltoids pressing down on me.

The feel of them in my hands.

Rocks.

Feel my breath changing.

Deeper, faster.

They're not my hands that are tracing my body.

They're his.

It's his that are undoing my trousers.

'Jayne –'

My name, his voice.

Over and over.

…

I'm shaking.

Thighs are twitching.

My ankles aching from being locked so tight.

They click as the tension escapes.

My eyes snap open.

'Jesus fucking Christ.'

Ten years, ten bloody years since I last had an orgasm.

And it wasn't like that.

Hellfire. Is that what it's always like?

My ankles click again.

Jesus fucking Christ.

—

Andrew's there waiting for me at the other side of the gates at Paddington Station.

He is in a navy suit, perfectly fitting to his shape.

We share a hug then leads me through the crowds and down onto the Tube.

I haven't been on the underground much before. We took the children here. Me and Malcolm. They would have been not much more than seven and nine.

And oh, Malcolm he didn't half moan all the way through the trip. Too dirty, too loud, too everything the city was to him.

I remember being on the Tube holding their little hands really tight, almost angry with them as I told them:

'Stay close. Don't you dare get lost now.'

Here we are now, Andrew's arm holding onto mine.

—

'We can go to a Pizza Express if you're feeling uncomfortable.'

He's guiding me round Brixton Market.

'Why'd I be feeling uncomfortable?'

'Culturally, perhaps this is more than you're used to.'

Three hours in, it's clearly dawning on Andrew that inviting me is the most massive mistake he's made. Polite chats done with, now we got nothing to say to each other, I'm boring old Mum.

'No. I want to see how you live, I want to see what's so good that you never come visit me.'

And I ignore him rolling his eyes, by pointing at the tiniest restaurant I've ever seen.

'We'll eat in here.'

'I don't think you'll like okonomiyaki.'

'You lived off waffles and beans until you were fourteen so let's not act like I'm the fussy eater.'

My elbow it's inches from two young women on the table to my left. We sit there in silence, both fiddling with our napkins. As we do, I can't help but listen to the girls talking about their weeks: about a terrible date one had with a man called Tobey.

'So did you enjoy your first couple of weeks retired?'

It's like Andrew's forgotten he's asked me that twice already.

'It has been lovely, actually.'

He nods.

'I've spent most of it masturbating.'

The young women next to us stop talking.

And after a while Andrew starts laughing, his whole face lights up.

And I do the same.

'About time, mother. About time.'

I smile at the girls next to me.

'It's true. Non-stop.'

'Sake!'

We talk, loudly. He asks what prompted this activity and I tell him about Deltoids. The sake it makes it a gigglier story than I realised:

'I woke up sticking to the sheets. I had to put them on a ninety-degree wash.'

We jump into a taxi and head across the river. All the buildings, Parliament, lit up before us. The light bouncing off them into the water.

'You know, this woman here, tonight, she's who I remember. From when I was a child. You used to make us laugh so much.'

'Did I?'

'Always so funny. That was who you were. Not a wife. Not a mother. You were you.'

Next morning, my son, he brings me a cup of tea in bed and cwtchs up next to me. We laugh and giggle as we scroll through the pictures on my phone piecing together our night: cocktails, a man in a leotard –

'Oh Andrew, please tell me that's my thumb over the phone!'

And he laughs, 'Doubtful' and then suddenly he goes:

'Let's go shopping.'

We're in Selfridges.

Alright, money bags. I'm saying to him as he tries to buy me a new pair of shoes.

I concede eventually and whilst he's off paying, I wander round the cosmetics. Floating on the aroma till I find myself stood before a counter. This bright-red lipstick staring back at me.

Back at his flat, my bags are all packed.

Andrew's not actually pushing me out the door, though, he's smiling.

'This hasn't been what I expected. I'm glad you found a reason to utilise a ninety-degree wash.'

'I actually got you a little something.' I'm holding up a Selfridges bag.

'For all the ones you stole.'

And as he's unwrapping it you can see the bemusement at what this could be and then it's just there.

A Christian Louboutin. Black pendant. Silky Satin Lipstick.

He shoves it back in the back, like it's red hot, then thrusts it back at me.

'What the fuck, Mum?'

'Andrew…?'

'Are you for real?

His lips are shaking, he's expecting something, I'm not sure what, but to be honest I've got no words coming, the shock of his anger, as he forces the bag back in my hand.

'You need to get going. You'll be alright doing the Tube yourself. Cross the road and then it's just round the corner. Change onto the Bakerloo line at Oxford Circus.'

He's not looking out from his flat window when I cross the road.

–

For two hours I stare at my phone, typing, deleting messages:

What did I do wrong, Andrew?

But by the time the train pulls back into Cardiff, I've not sent a thing and I'm no closer to figuring it out.

In the taxi home, the drive is telling me how he is really pleased with his new hybrid car. How quiet it is.

Truth is, everything seems so quiet in Cardiff. I never seen it that way before. Only city I ever lived.

The taxi pulls up Torrens Drive and I see my house.

'What?!'

'You alright?' The drive asks me.

'Can you just pull in here.' I don't wait for any change, it's fine I tell him.

I start walking up the hill, wheelie suitcase alongside me.

'Evening, Gill.'

She is there just walking off my path and for a moment, she's like a rabbit in the headlight before it is all smiles.

'Evening, I didn't recognise you there.'

I smiles back.

'Oh, I do like your shoes, are they new?'

'They are.'

We're at a crossroads now because to get off my path she'd have to walk past me. Gill fidgets slightly, looks at my wheelie suitcase.

'Been away, have you?'

'I have. London'

'Oh, the devil's town.'

'Bit harsh, Gill.'

I look over her shoulder, I can see my wheelie bin is not quite where I left it.

'Was there anything I could do for you?' I am all smiles as I ask her.

'Oh. No… I wasn't in when a parcel was delivered earlier, thought they might have tried you, obviously not though. I should leave you to unpack.'

And I take in the night.

'Did you try looking in your wheelie bin, Gill, they often do that.'

'That's a good idea, I didn't, I'll do that now.'

And Gill, she really does try to start making a move this time.

'Might as well try mine whilst you're here, never know.'

'Erm.'

I'm still all smiles as I walk towards my bin: 'You just never know, do you, Gill.' Weird things is, she actually follows me, like I have cast a spell on her.

I opens the bin up.

'Oh, that's funny, no parcel, but my bin's all full, wasn't like that when I left.'

'No?'

'No, Gill.'

I lift up the top bin bag and take outs the one below.

'See that, not one of my bags, got no yellow tie. I only ever use the one with yellow ties see. Must be someone else's. Imagine doing that.'

Gill is silent.

'Why don't you take it back, Gill. Because I'll be needing that space for myself you see.'

I watch her walk back with the bag up to her house. Give her a little wave as she looks back. And she sort of copies.

No messages on my phone when I look at it.

'I'm back safe.'

A kiss too, I send to Andrew.

Two WhatsApp ticks go blue. A thumbs up arrives two hours later.

–

It is bucketing down, apocalyptic, yet all I'm thinking about is Deltoids in the park.

On the Saturday night, Andrew had been insistent that I go down on Monday.

I thought he might follow it up, remind me, push me to do it.

But no, all I've stills got is the thumbs up from last night.

Clara and Jacob are fighting me as I am there shoving them both into the pram.

Barely a yard I can see ahead of us.

I looks like a mad woman, pushing a double buggy around the lake, not another soul in site, even the ducks and swans taking shelter – but I keeps going and the children, they are crying now.

'Nanny we want to go home!'

But we're there now. At the top of the promenade. Looking down into the playground.

And of course it is empty.

Of course it is.

I goes to myself: what are you thinking?

Stood there.

Children crying.

All sodden.

Stupid, stupid woman.

…

Then a car it beeps its horn.

There.

Parked by the gates, on the road, is a big-long car.

And stood by the door is a man with shoulders.

Jet-black brolly above him.

Alun.

'Give you a lift somewhere.'

…

Next thing we are parked outside my house.

'This you then, is it.'

'Yeah.'

'Handy. For the park.'

'Yeah.'

…

'Why don't you come in?'

…

The engine stops.

–

The kids pile into the front room.

I give them snacks, some warm milk.

Us both a cup of tea.

And Clara asks, I say asks, demands a film.

So I put a film on for them.

Toy Story.

We watch them for a little bit, all huddled up together on the sofa, as we sips our tea.

My feet are sodden, so I say: I'm just going to the bedroom… to change my socks.

And then I heads upstairs.

Off the socks go, and I just stand there, feet on carpet, socks in hand…

Waiting…

I hear the baby gate click and then his footsteps coming up the stairs.

I step out onto the landing.

He's there.

Something happens.

Something I'm transmitting which makes him stop.

My heart's beating so hard.

'Absorbed. Not a peep from them,' he goes.

'Good.'

The floorboards creak slightly.

From me, it is me that is moving, not Alun. I step into him.

We are inches away.

Faces, bodies, mouths.

I drop my socks.

I take his arms, pull him that final inch into me.

I reach for his shoulders.

I trace his deltoids.

Grip them, rocks in my hands.

It is not a nest I am after.

I want to be devoured.

There, on my landing, we are kissing.

I am kissing a man, who is kissing me back.

Nothing else exists.

Just us connected.

I pull him tighter into me.

His hand slips under my jumper, caresses the base of my spine.

Every single hair on my body stands on end.

My hips press into him.

I can feel he wants me.

I stop kissing him.

And I have to tell him:

'…Alun… it's been a long time since, I don't know if I can… practically… I want to…'

He stops me with a smile.

'Jayne, what do *you* want?'

…

'My name, say it again.'

'Jayne –'

(*Deep breath.*)

'Jayne –'

I unbuckle my jeans, take his hand.

There?

Yes.

I reach into his trousers.

'Jayne'

Yes

'Jayne'

There

'Jayne'

That

'Jayne'

Exact

'Jayne'

Spot.

…

We sit on the top of the stairs afterwards, getting our breaths back.

I can see his cum is running down one of the ridges in the anaglypta. He spots it too. We both start to laugh.

'Jayne, they need to prescribe you on the NHS, I've not had a hard-on like that since I was a teenager. Seriously, I've had to take the little blue pill to get the party started last times I've tried.'

He's not embarrassed, he seems completely at peace.

I kiss him, firmly.

'More where that came from.'

'I hope so.'

I rest my head on his shoulders, he rests his head gently onto mine.

Hands like this, finding each other.

We listen to the sounds of Buzz Lightyear and Woody navigating their way to life lasting friendship downstairs.

'Nanny, it's finished!'

Clara's voice snaps us back.

'I can do us all some lunch, or do you have to go?'

'No, we don't have to go.'

–

When Alun leaves I feel helpless, but it is a minute earlier than planned that he calls.

'I couldn't wait', he tells me.

I'm there listening to his voice, I start getting hot and –

So I tell him this.

I tell him to say what he'd do if he was here right now.

And as he does, I catch myself in a mirror.

My reflection

It's like I don't recognise myself.

Hands down my jeans

Touching myself.

And you know what, I loves what I see.

–

The Monday phone ritual passes with no call from Andrew, it slipped my mind truth be told.

A text later: 'sorry, got held up.'

'As long as you're alright,' I text him back.

He's not asked for an update on Alun so I keep him and our antics as my dirty secret.

I'm going to his house on Friday for the weekend. It would be sooner but he's still working three days a week. Consulting in Bristol.

I make it very clear to him that the plan is to have sex.

Six thirty he picks me up.

My wheelie bag all packed.

'Don't worry, it's full of lubricant not clothes.'

'Jayne. Get in the car now.'

He lives up near Caerleon, it's somewhere he'd been renting since he got back from the Emirates. Never found anywhere after his divorce. But that he liked the views.

'Views.'

It's like one of them paintings you see, you know where someone's travelled miles upon miles just to capture it.

'Beautiful.'

I take his hand and gesture to take me into his house.

He puts music on.

We drink wine, laugh.

Kiss like teenagers on his sofa.

I tell him I'm going to the bathroom, then I'm going to get into his bed.

Fresh sheets.

Never known a man do that before.

Malcolm he'd just pile his clothes beside the bed and like magic they'd just appear in his wardrobe all fresh and ironed.

'Jayne, you alight there?'

'Alun, my head wants this, very badly. My body might just need some extra assistance. Accommodating.'

'Well that can be a lot of fun, finding ways to accommodate.'

And I'm staring at this man, looking at me with such hunger that I can't help but feel completely alive.

I open the wheelie case. Remove two bottles of Durex Play Perfect Glide.

'You weren't joking when you said it was full of lubricant.'

'Buy one, get one free. Woman in Boots was ever so helpful.'

'That's a lot of action.'

'Well, we got a lot of time to make up for.'

I dim the lights.

Beckon him over.

We unbutton each other's clothes as we kiss.

We duck under the duvet, only our underwear left on.

I go to undo my bra.

'Can I do that, Jayne?'

And I let him.

He works his way down my body.

No prompting.

It's what he wants.

My knickers are gone now.

Fuck, I'm naked.

Wow.

Oh wow.

This is very new.

Attention there.

With his tongue.

Suddenly I realise my thighs are squeezing his neck.

'Sorry, sorry, Alun, can you breathe?!'

'I like it, I'll tap if it's too much.'

He doesn't tap. And my ankle clicks. Again. And then again.

He fits very nicely in my mouth. It's so empowering being in utter control of his pleasure.

'I have a condom.'

'Hate to break it to you, Alun, but I'm a bit late in life to be getting pregnant.'

I coat him in the lubricant.

He's on top of me.

I guide him in with my hand.

I breathe deep.

Close my eyes.

My hands grip into his back.

Pulling him in tighter.

…

'Next time, I promise it will last longer.'

We both burst into laughter.

'Honestly, that was lovely.'

And I can't just lie there, there's so much energy charging through my body and then I hear it calling me:

'Where you going, Jayne?'

And he's following me naked through his house till it stops me:

Music.

Still playing from earlier.

'I love this song.'

And I turn it up and let it soak into my bones.

Turn that down, that's what Malcolm he'd be saying. Turn it fucking down, woman.

Fuck him, eh. Fuck him.

'You like dancing, then, Jayne?'

'I love it.'

'Oh, I got two left feet...'

I don't care, I don't need you to dance with me, Alun.

...

For years all I wished is for time to speed up.

Now it does.

Monday night he takes me out for a curry.

I'm not a fan, but it's Alun's favourite so I go along, polite, right?

The next Friday, he only goes and brings me some gifts.

Underwear.

All lace and colour.

'I can't wear these.'

'Oh yes, you can.'

And so, you know what, I do.

Not just with him, everywhere.

Days later I head into town on the bus and the satin in my knickers shifts.

…the feel of them.

Invigorating.

I look around the bus at all the passengers, all so bored, and you know what I think: I think if only you knew that teeth had pulled them down my thighs last Saturday night.

It's like I'm hooked.

My wardrobe, my drawers.

Everything gets emptied.

If it doesn't give me that feeling I'm not interested.

Aisles I never stepped down in Marks' I'm raiding, you know the ones, all the colours all the fabrics.

And I look myself over in the mirror, I think back to Malcolm in that last year:

'Could at least try, Jayne. Coming home to that, not leaving me much to get excited about, are you.'

Fuck off!

–

'Mam, you got a prostitute staying with you?'

Emma's shouting from upstairs.

'It's like a tart's boudoir up here.'

She's pointing at my laundry, it's all on a rack drying in Andrew's old room.

'No, that's mine. I met someone.'

'I see.'

'Alun.'

'Okay. And those are what you are wearing, are they? For Alun.'

'No, I'm wearing them for me.'

She's grimacing, like she's popped a lemon into her mouth.

'What?'

'Not got the time, Mam, I've got to get the kids home.'

'No, go on say it, Emma.'

…

…

'Mam, they're not really appropriate for you, are they.'

–

The waiters topping up our glasses.

'Got a nice little bit of heat to it this one.'

Alun's pointing at his dhaba lamb.

I'm not really paying attention, my knickers feel like they're biting into me. My phone's ringing.

'Going to get that, Jayne?'

'Are you okay, Mam?

'Been speaking to your sister, have you, Andrew? Going to laugh at me too, is it? Not calling, joking at my expense behind my back.'

'Stop. Please. All I want to know is, are you happy, Mam?'

Alun's there in the Empire's window, taking a big bite of his naan.

'I don't know.'

It's quiet for a second, just a motorbike racing down the road filling the air.

'When you want me to meet him, you tell me and I'll come.'

–

Next morning when I come downstairs Alun's washing up our coffee mugs. I watch him put them in the cupboard that for the last twenty years I've used for glasses.

'Stop that, will you.'

He dries his hands on the tea towel.

'Am I a dirty secret?'

'What you on about, Jayne?'

Have you told your children about me?'

'I have.'

'Why have I not met them then? I know one lives in Bilbao, but Julia, she's only round the corner, her daughter is in my house all the time.'

Men they'd rather live in silence, right. They'd just rather bury their heads in the sand, yeah. And I can tell Alun's fighting that instinct. Finally, he finishes drying his hands.

'I wasn't a good dad. So it's taken a long time for my girls to trust me. And I like how you see me.'

He's back fiddling with the tea towel, so I take it off him.

'We got a lot a ghosts at our age, haven't we.'

He nods.

'I know you're not perfect, Alun. Taking it upon yourself to move where my bloody mugs and glasses go.'

'It makes more sense to have the glasses by – '

'Not to me.'

'Well, why didn't you say?'

'I am now. So, when am I meeting them then?'

—

I meet Julia in Coffee Number One on Wellfield Road.

'My dad tells me you're a good dancer, Jayne, good luck with old concrete feet here.'

And Alun sorts of disappears into the sofa as we get lost having a joke at his expense.

—

A week later it is my turn.

Emma initiated it, she actually stopped for a cup of tea rather than just racing off when she collected the kids.

'We're having a little gathering for my birthday next Sunday. Bring Alun if you like.'

I asked him if he'd be alright with that. After all Malcolm would be there.

'I'm a big boy, Jayne.'

'Yes, you are.'

Andrew comes up the night before.

I stick my head in through the doorway to his old room later.

He's there tracing his finger along the side of his old wardrobe.

Beckons me over.

Guides my finger along it.

'Used a compass. My countdown.'

I feel the side of the wardrobe, it's covered in notches.

'School wasn't easy for me.'

His eyes are a little blurry from the bottle of the wine, we've drank.

'It made you the success you are.'

'Fuck's sake, Mam, that's not the point is it.'

–

Alun parks up next to the Jaguar.

Can't really hear much noise coming from inside when we ring the bell.

Dave answers, big bottle of bubbly in his hand.

'Perfect timing!'

Now, not to boast but Alun is looking very handsome. A lovely polo shirt. Deltoids really on show. I watch the shape of him as he follows Dave through the house, nodding each time Dave tells him what work they've had done.

'There was a wall here.'

Penny's laughing in the kitchen.

'Your mum and Alun are here, Em.'

Alun pauses, sticks his hand out, I catch up with him and take it.

Then we step through into the kitchen.

It's not much of a party, it's just the two children, Emma, Malcolm, Andrew and –

'Hi', it's Penny, her smile so big, surprised it's not cracking her face.

'This is… Alun?'

It's the deltoids, she's got her eyes on them.

'Hi.' Alun says.

'Hi Penny.' I go.

'Hi Jayne… you look… very well.'

'I'm feeling well too, actually.'

Malcolm's up now.

Me and Penny watch them shake hands.

She's glancing at me.

Very confused.

And do you know what, I can't help but smile.

–

'Where are all Emma's friends?' I ask Dave as he tops up my glass.

'She's doing something with... you know... Carrie, from school, next week.'

Emma's there on autopilot slicing pizza for the children.

She never really saw me with friends. Girls from school, I left them behind when I moved to Cyncoed. The women I met there, when I got divorced they all disappeared.

'Do you want me to do that?' I say to her about the pizzas.

'It's okay, I got it. Go and mingle.'

She's gesturing towards her father and Alun.

As I head over, I hear Alun saying that he lives in Caerleon.

'Close to the Celtic Manor,' Malcolm goes.

'You a golfer, Alun?'

'Well, I own some clubs.'

'Very tricky, the courses up at the Celtic Manor. You played them?'

'Once or twice.'

'I found places like St Mellons were much better for *those* starting out. *Those* with higher handicaps. Did you play enough to get a handicap, Alun?'

'Yeah, I did.'

Malcolm's leaning in, with that smug old smile of his, waiting...

'I got to two. When I was playing a lot, now I'd be lucky to play off ten. How about yourself?'

And Malcolm's not smiling any more he's fiddling with his glass. Now I don't know anything about golf, but I know from Malcolm's reaction that what Alun just said is very impressive.

'What are we talking about here?'

Penny joins us all smiles.

I can't help it – it just comes out. 'Golf handicaps!'

'Oh, has he been boasting again? Not been able to get him to shut up about it.'

'They don't need to hear.'

'Yes, they do. Fifteen, he has finally got to. The number of hours and lessons… you were so delighted, weren't you.'

Malcolm's jaw is twitching, and again I can't help myself, I have to ask, even though I know:

'Is fifteen better than two?'

'Oh god, no. He dreams of a number like that. Don't you?'

–

Dave playfully pokes Emma in the stomach, as she blows out her candles.

'Not many places had a cake big enough to fit them all on.'

'Thanks, you're such a poet, Dave. Could you cut it, Mam?'

I cut the cake into slices and watch as Emma disappears upstairs.

I take a piece over to Malcolm. I look at a photo of Emma and Dave from their wedding day. She looked so happy.

'Does Emma seem…?'

'What?'

'Tired.'

'Well, she does have a full-time job, Jayne. I can tell you, it's very stressful working those hours.'

'Nanny, can I show you my painting of a lion eating Jacob?'

Clara's got hold of my hand.

'Can Grandad see it too?'

'No, just Nanny.'

We leave Malcolm drinking his drink.

–

'Oh'

Emma goes, when I tell her me and Alun have decided to go away for Christmas.

'It's your turn with Dave's family this year. And your brother's jet-setting with his friends.'

I loved the idea of some winter sun, like Andrew too, you know lounger by the sea, but in the end it turns out my passport is out of date so we book a little cottage in the Peak District.

On Christmas Eve we walk to the pub in the rain, overlooking this viaduct, that stretches for miles and miles.

'We can travel, do anything you know.'

–

It is a sunny Friday at the end of January. We are all at the swings. Alun, me, the three children.

'Alun, I think we have become a bit of a source of gossip.'

Because a few mums keep smiling at us. It's as if our romance has become their soap opera. We are what they gossip about with their coffees after.

'Ah, isn't it so sweet, I bet they say. I tell you what, girls, there's times when there is nothing sweet about what we get up to, oh no. We are animals.'

I am expecting a laugh, from Alun, about what I just said, but nothing.

So I say it again. And he looks at me this time.

'I need to move to Bilbao.'

...

Clara's swing just hits me in the leg.

'Jayne.'

I'm not hearing the words he's saying properly, just bits, phrases.

Words like: Abby needs help. Her husband just diagnosed with cancer.

Because I'm having an out a body experience:

I'm up above the lake, floating, looking down on the oaks and pines, suddenly there's a gust of a wind and I'm being blown, far away from the swings below, over the houses, and I don't want to be there, I want to be back where I was –

'Jayne. Do you understand what I'm asking you?'

Alun's hand is on my arms, stopping me drifting away.

'I want you to come with me. What do you say, Jayne?'

I say...

I say...

–

'Bilbao, is this a joke'?

'No, Em. So, what do you think?'

Emma's walking out of the kitchen, calling the children, pushing them towards the front door.

'Emma? Emma? Emma?!'

'Mam, I can't believe you'd do this.'

'Do this?'

...

Emma's biting her lip with such force, I'm expecting any second blood to come spurting out.

'Do you even know where Bilbao is?'

'It's in the Basque region of Northern Spain.'

That stops her a little:

'…Curries… yeah curries! You, you, hate them, but that's what you eat because he likes it. Can't you see it, Mam, you're being shaped by him. You're not being you.'

'Who am I then? Who am *I*, Emma?'

'Ow, Mammy.'

It's Clara, her hand being gripped too tight by Emma.

'You are my mam. When Dad left you didn't fight for him, but you said you'd always fight for me though, that you'd always be there for me.'

–

Alun's stood just in front of me.

The deltoids it is like they've been deflated.

'Say it, Jayne.'

'Alun… Emma, I can't leave her, the children, she needs me.'

Last bit of air escapes.

He rubs his face.

Smiles at me.

'Oh, Jayne.'

–

Love is unconditional with children, it is not something you can stop, right.

Romance it dies.

It dies.

…?

…

It is three weeks now since he went.

…

I…

I'd been so silly. The underwear, the sex, it wasn't me.

It wasn't…

…

I was in the park last Monday and one of the mams came up to me and asked me if I was okay.

I…

She said me, Clara and Jacob could join them for coffee.

I…

…

–

'I'm coming back to see you.'

It's Andrew on my voicemail.

And there he is Friday night nine p.m. bottle of wine in his hand.

He pours two glasses, sits me down on the sofa and he stares at me. He takes a deep breath then calmly tells me, that he loves me but that what I did hurt him.

'The lipstick. Of all the things to buy me.'

'But you used to always love taking mine.'

'And how did that play out, Mam. How did that game end?'

My stomach drops. I'm trying not to let the moment come back to me but it's still so clear in my head:

Andrew, sixteen, there in me and Malcolm's old bedroom, looking at me, tears streaming. His lips bright red with my lipstick. His father shouting at him.

'Wipe that shit off.'

And Andrew, he's waiting, waiting for me to say something. But I don't. Instead I'm racing to the make-up table, grabbing tissues, trying to wipe it off, and slowly all the fights goes from him and I'm just gripping, rubbing his face as Malcolm points at me:

'You made him this.'

I just kept wiping and wiping.

'Mam, I know you remember this. I know you do.'

'Right. Shut up, shut up, Andrew! Do you reckon you'd be a management consultant or whatever it is you do for a living in London, if you grew up in Rumney? Or Emma, be living up in Lisvane in a million-pound house?

'What the fuck are you talking about, Mother?'

'Cos you wouldn't, you'd be like your cousins, grafting in Home Bargains on minimum wage, and living like my sister, in that house *you* hated visiting.

That day, you want to talk about that day, fine: I knew your father wanted to leave me. I couldn't have you go back to where I grew up, because you think he'd just give me the house in Cyncoed? Support me, no. So, yeah, I took his side. I was doing what was best for you.

Andrew's up on his feet muttering what sounds like martyr, fucking martyr.

'What you saying?'

And he looks me dead in the eye.

'Martyr. You are a fucking martyr. Mam, you didn't have to stay round here for us.'

'I did, you had school here.'

'That hellhole? I was never as lonely in my life as I was then, and you know that.'

'My father he wronged you no doubt, but be honest, it was you that didn't want to go back to that life. It was you that didn't want to go back to that house in Rymney. So don't blame me for you fucking up when I needed you the most.'

He necks his drink. Tops it up. Mine too.

'I know you had a lot fucking going on, but so did I! Sorry, sorry, it's just if I don't say this now I never will.

'Andrew. No, stop, no. You do not apologise, I am your mam, I wasn't what you needed. I am sorry. Andrew, I am sorry.'

We sip our drinks.

'I've got a good life now, I love being a *strategy* consultant.'

He puts his arm around me. I lean into him.

'They fuck us up, parents, don't they.'

'Yeah, I'd say my father did most of that though.'

He kisses my head.

'But at least I know where I got my being a snob from. Do you want to go with Alun?'

'Even if I did, I can't leave Emma.'

He makes me follow his eyes, around the room, at pictures of her on her wedding day, her children... 'She's already left. Mam, you got one life, that's all, just one.'

—

'What you doing here?'

Emma's got Jacob asleep, clutched to her chest.

'Can we talk inside?'

'What's this about? Dave's playing golf, and I've got to collect Clara from ballet in half an hour.'

'I don't think you're happy, Emma. No shame in it, I'm not happy.'

'Jesus, I don't have time for this, you've got Facebook, if you want an outlet for your melodrama.'

Now she's trying to walk away trying to get through to the kitchen, but I won't let her, I'm blocking her path and everything starts coming out a lot clearer than I imagine, because I'm saying I didn't know if I wanted to go with Alun, but she guilted me into not having a choice.

'That's not true at all.'

'It is, Em.'

Oh god, Mam, he's just some man.'

'He's not just some man, Emma. I love him.'

Jacob starts wriggling in her arms.

'Like you got a clue what love is, Mam.'

'Darling, I'm going to need you to take that back.'

'Oh god, how is it me that is having to tell you this, you're confusing lust, with love. He just wants you to go out there and look after him and his family. You'd just be in his service.'

'Service? What do you even need me for? I mean actually need, darling. What is it that you can get from me that you couldn't just get from a nursery? I'm childcare that's all I am to you.'

'That's not true.'

'It is, Emma. You don't respect me, darling. Never have, that's fine. Truth is, I don't think you even like me, let alone love me. So don't stand there telling me I don't have a clue what love is.'

She's looking at anywhere but me, the floor, ceiling, plasma television.

'Don't like you... Mam, I... don't... respect you... that's what... you think...?'

'Yeah, and right now I resent you, and if I don't get a chance to try this for myself, I worry that I will end up hating you.'

It starts slowly.

This noise.

Low.

It's sobbing.

'Emma, Emma?'

She can't stop though.

Every second it's growing.

Now it's a wail.

'I'm a failure. Failure, failure, failure…'

'No, you're not, darling.'

'I am. I'm failing in everything.'

'That's not true.'

'It is. They call out for you at night, they, they, I lose my temper with them all the time, I called Jacob a shitty little rat twice yesterday, and my colleagues don't trust me, they think I'm incapable, the joke, I'm failing, as a worker, as a mother, as a daughter, as a woman. I am a failure.'

And for a second there's a gap, it's like, you know, she's reached the end but then this second wind comes and now Jacob joins in and I take him from her.

'And Dave's useless. He's useless. Can't even turn the dishwasher on. He just sits there, tells me how tough his day was, drinks a bottle of wine, watches the golf. He drinks so much, so so much. Oh god, I married my fucking father.'

And do you know what, she actually laughs. Real proper laughing. And so do I.

'Dad thought changing one nappy made him a hero, he still talks about it.'

'Well, he is a bit of an arsehole.'

And Emma's nodding, 'I know, I know, then why do I still need his approval?'

I take her hand.

'Because he didn't just leave me. He left you too.

'But why?'

This sits in the room.

I look around her immaculate house.

'Look, your father has many faults. But if I'm being honest, I never loved him, Emma, not like I do with Alun. And your father, he did love me at the beginning, he so wanted me to love him. But deep down I never felt it. Which must have worn away at him. And I think Penny does love him, so yeah, I played my part.'

Emma squeezes my hand.

'You just gave us everything.'

'Well maybe I shouldn't have. Maybe I should have been more selfish. Who knows. Nobody gets being a parent right.'

On cue Jacob's nappy starts leaking out the sides.

'I want to be a better person, Mam, I'm just so tired. So, so tired.'

'I know, I know.'

'I'm scared. You've always been there for me. Always. I don't want you to hate me.'

I open my arms and she folds into me.

'I hate curries, Em.'

'Then tell him, Mam.'

...

Fucking hell, my legs are shaking

And I grab my phone.

It rings.

Another ring.

And he picks up –

'I hate curries, Alun. If I'm coming, I don't want to eat them.'

'It's all tapas here, Jayne.'

'And I'm not giving up my life here. I'd be coming back and forth. I want to be with my family too.'

'Sounds great, Jayne.'

–

Malcolm pulls up. Him and Penny look like they've aged thirty years as the kids squeeze out of the back of the Jaguar.

'Go through.' I tell them as they zoom through into the house.

He's ruffling his hair, Malcolm is.

'Bloody hell, knackering that. Them.'

'Yeah.'

'I was away a lot, wasn't I, when ours were that age.'

'It kept a roof over our head.'

'This is you then, is it?'

'This is what your children learnt to call home.'

'Touché.'

The man next to me, together, we made them. My kids. Whatever happened after, it was worth it.

Penny gently breaks the moment.

'Have a lovely time in Bilbao, Jayne.'

I study her, this face I hated. Do you know what, it's much gentler than I realised. Needier maybe. And when I hug her, it feels a lot more natural than I expected. Malcolm's clearly confused watching us hold each other. Definitely relieved when we eventually let go.

'Go. Enjoy the peace.'

I watch them speed away.

—

Emma invites me round for Sunday lunch.

'Can't promise you won't get poisoned. Dave's cooking.'

And when I get there, he's watching the golf whilst he peels the potatoes.

'They go in for – '

'I got it all under control. Sit down, Em.'

She curls up next to me on the sofa.

'We'll give you a lift to the airport.'

'I can get a taxi.'

'No, we can give you a lift.'

Emma shifts her head onto my shoulder.

'Are you all packed?'

'I've got a week left yet, Em.'

'Was just thinking we could do a bit of shopping together, before, you know.'

'I'd like that.'

Jacob and Clara come running in. Jump on us both.

'Can we put *Hey Duggee* on?'

'What do you say?'

'Now??'

Emma laughs, as she scoops up Clara onto her lap.

'Pleaaaaaase!'

The channel changes. Clara and Jacob disappear into it. Dave puts the potatoes in the oven. Comes and sits down too.

'Roly he's my favourite.' On cue. Roly does something that makes Jacob laugh so much he farts.

We watch for a little while. Emma strokes Clara's hair.

'You know that Nanny's going to be going away for a little while.'

'Is it an adventure, Nanny?'

I stroke her hair too. My fingers hook into Emma's. Duggee woofs.

'Yeah, that's the plan.'

End.

IDYLL

Acknowledgements

Deepest thanks to Elle While, Sophie Motley, Harry Egan and the entire Pentabus team. I had the privilege of growing up in a village similar to the one in this play, so thanks to all those I went to school and grew up with for their unwitting inspiration, and of course my wife, daughter and family.

M.H.

Idyll was first produced by Pentabus and performed at Stokesay Court, Onibury, on 18 August 2021 before touring. The company was as follows:

Performer	Harry Egan
Director	Elle While
Designer	Lucy Sierra
Sound Designer	Dan Balfour
Lighting Designer	James Mackenzie
Assistant Director	Alessandra Davison
Associate Sound Designer	Dylan Winn-Davies
Production Manager	Fiona Hilton
Stage Manager	Kirsty Smith

The performer welcomes people, smiles hello, it's informal, friendly. When ready...

THE STORY

Hello.

I want you to imagine you are looking at a map.

An Ordnance Survey map.

If it helps close your eyes. I promise I won't use this as a chance to steal your bags and do a runner, leaving you with your eyes closed for fifty minutes.

Now, you can feel the map in your hand.

You can hear it crinkling as you unfold it, as you spread it out, onto your lap, your desk, your car bonnet, your...

(*A gesture, whatever you'd do it on.*)

Key thing is, this is not Google Earth, it's not Street View. Not on your phone or computer.

You are not zooming in to see if it really is a swimming pool in *that* back garden.

It is paper.

It is tangible.

Real.

It has a universal language. Symbols that as you recognise them tell you a story of the land.

Of its geography.

Now, if you are that person who unfolds the whole map out.

Takes up all the space around you, or what you have spread it out on.

(*They demonstrate the act.*)

We all know that person, might even be sat next to them. They will be a man.

Well curb your natural instincts – less in this case is definitely more.

What is in front of you is a map that is about eight squares across and twelve upwards – sounds like I'm describing a game of battleships – imagine the size of *Countrylife* – is that a useful reference?

A magazine. A4 paper.

And not to be patronising, sure you all do know, but in case my sister is here, each of those squares equates to one kilometre.

So, what you are looking at is an area that is eight kilometres east to west, twelve south to north.

Now as you look at this section of the map what you are seeing is a lot of green.

That is your first impression.

Green and various shades of it.

And in case it wasn't clear what all this green represented, hundreds of minute little sketches of trees fill large swathes of it.

The other predominant colour is white. Huge swathes of white.

Resting within all of this, taking up almost one square, in the centre of this page, is a light-blue circle. Not perfect. Imagine a small child has attempted to draw a circle – that is the shape.

From there a blue line snakes its way down till it leaves just east of the centre of the map.

You know by looking at the map there are no major roads in this area.

It is a land of B roads; of bends and turns, of walls and hedgerows sometimes higher than the car itself.

The contours on the map and the gaps between them tell you that this is an area of peaks and troughs. Of dips and sways.

You know by looking that this is a place where the idea of rolling mobile phone coverage is non-existent.

You know that a primary school closed recently because it was deemed unviable.

You know that a bus only stops along the routes twice a day rather than the six it once did.

But you also know that it is beautiful. And every day animals roam and fill the land with their own laughter and song.

You know that the area changes colours throughout the year, dark reds and oranges of autumn, the bright dazzling yellow of spring.

And you know that it is these qualities that make people visit it from all over the world and stare at the houses and hills and fields and streams and woods – its silence – and dream of living in such a place.

Now I want you to focus on two squares.

East 3 and 4. South 2.

This is the second largest village on the map.

If by looking at its sprawl and the sketchings for houses, you had guessed a population of five hundred people, you should buy a lottery ticket tonight, as the official population at the last census was five hundred and seven.

Now as you really study these two squares, you can see several symbols: a blue tankard, a cross and on its outskirts a wigwam.

Now. If they were still closed, open your eyes.

Those two squares: that is where we are now.

That is where this story takes place.

Over the course of a morning, on a scorching July day.

Now whilst a map can create a picture of the land, it does not really tell you about the people who live in it.

Their tics, their traits.

Or the stories that unfold around them.

So that is what I am here to do.

I am going to bring them and the story to life.

Okay.

Ready.

Let us begin:

–

Gunshots shatter the early morning silence.

'Missed the dirty bastard!'

Harry Bailey has been at war with a rabbit for months.

'He's pitched a tent in the back garden, he says he's not sleeping in the house until it's dead.'

That is Diane, his wife, she had been telling this to Madeline Booth on the phone the night before.

'Embrace it, Di. Enjoy the peace, all that lovely space in your bed.'

'Way past that, he's been in the spare room for two months now.'

'Oh Diane.'

'Truth is, it's been coming for a long time. He's feral, he's lost it.'

A dramatic gasp, you'd think Madeline had seen a ghost.

(*Acts it out.*)

'Goodness, did you see that, Di?'

'What?'

'Lights flickering up in the woods, on the hill.'

Although at opposite ends of the village, Madeline and Diane both have a view of the woods from their front windows.

'Can you see it, up on the top?'

'...No.'

'I swear I just saw lights going off. My eyes, maybe, I shouldn't have had that fifth gin.'

They talk for the duration of two more gins. Over the last eighteen years these gin and chats have become a ritual. The phone currently replacing their living rooms or gardens or The Red Lion's snug, a friendship that neither saw coming when Diane and Harry had moved here nineteen years ago: the tourists that visited and fell in love with a village so much they moved there to raise their children.

And Madeline, the local who sold them her house when her children left home.

Twice more Madeline thought she saw lights flicker in the woods but put it aside to encourage Di to vent.

See, Harry is a fifty-four-year-old accountant. Head of a firm. Historically, his days have always been filled with lots of people popping in asking for his guidance in the office.

'Harry, do you have a sec? Got a question about the Hull-Baileys account.'

'Sure, take a seat.'

His day used to consist of three hours commuting. Five live, on the way in. Beatles and Pink Floyd on the way back. Lately though he has had all that time back. Working from home, he has had no one popping into his office to ask for advice.

(*For a moment we are Harry, waiting at his computer desk – nothing.*)

With so much more time on his hands gardening has taken over. Strawberries being his most treasured crop and it's these strawberries that have become the target for the rabbit.

The gunshot woke up several people.

The chain of dog barks that followed woke up several more.

Alice Rose takes it as a sign to get out of bed.

Like most that heard it, the gunshot did not fill her with fear. It is a sound that she is used to, that often rings round the hills.

Looking at the light that is fighting through the gaps in the curtains Alice can tell that today is going to be another hot day.

Paul, her boyfriend of nine years, is still fast asleep, so she doesn't open them. She throws on some clothes, sticks her head into Carly, her eight-year-old's bedroom – still fast asleep – then heads downstairs to let Ralph out.

'On the grass, not the paving.'

Too late. The wee trickles down the patio towards the doorstep.

'Thought Labradors were meant to be obedient' Alice mutters as she rubs Ralph's ears.

Alice's phone beeps, a WhatsApp message.

There is a point we all have had when a phone beeps, where our heart skips, hope.

Is it?

And in this case, it is.

She reads the message. And despite herself a smile breaks across her face.

'Come on, Ralph.'

Alice's house is in the middle of the village. One of twelve that was built in a little cul-de sac in the seventies as part of the government's drive for more council property.

It was Paul's dad's house. He bought it in the eighties and left it to Paul when he died, four years ago. It is the only house that Paul has ever lived in. When Alice discovered she was expecting a baby at seventeen it made sense for her to move in with Paul and his dad. And it has been where she has lived ever since but...

Where was I... sun through curtains... hot...

Hot days have been frequent of late.

At first it was a welcome relief.

The smell of barbecues in back gardens'.

Cooling dips by the shallow banks of the river.

Long nights sat on patios and deckchairs watching the darkness and stars arriving.

A welcome distraction from the chaos unfolding around the world.

But the relentlessness of heat, the continual inescapability of it, the lack of sleep those hot nights bring.

It creates edge, right.

Suffocating.

Everyone becomes angsty, tired, tempers are quicker to fray –

You definitely know what I mean –

The sun stops becoming that welcoming relief. Every person can be heard muttering:

'We need a storm – that will break it – cool everyone down'

and every day that passes without a storm arriving, the tension builds and builds and builds.

Add to this heat every villager has the knowledge that another hot day brings more of the same:

Visitors.

See these scorching days brought a pattern. A pattern that many in the village quickly tired of.

Noise.

Cars.

Day-trippers.

The villagers quickly finding it was no longer just their personal sanctuary but one for those from far and wide as well.

'Invasion, vermin, each of them, who knows what they've got, can't let them in.'

Joey Belk had not been afraid to write that on the village's Facebook group.

And he was not alone in the sentiment.

Sixty-three likes. Quite a lot of smiley faces.

And in a private WhatsApp group for The Red Lion's darts team, he had set about plans to tack the village's roads, to pierce the tyres of the cars that were descending.

This has been shot down when it was pointed out to him:

'End up puncturing our own tyres, you moron.'

Instead, they had settled on the idea of setting up a roadblock at the entrance of the village to keep people out.

And that's where Joey is off to when his truck speeds past Alice and Ralph.

'He's harmless, just denser than lead,' Paul would always laugh and say about Joey to Alice.

Every village has a Joey.

Louder than all others.

Uncensored.

The 'knobhead'.

He, she, they, but let's be honest he, is probably missing a finger, or a tooth, walks with a limp – an injury of some sort from doing something involving alcohol.

Joey is missing a nipple.

One night in The Red Lion they were drinking lit sambucas and what was meant to happen is that after knocking it back the drinkers would put a hand over the glass – the idea being that the heat would cause a vacuum, leaving the glass stuck to whoever's hand. Joey upped the ante. He necked his shot and then pressed the glass over his nipple – but the trick really only works if you'd made sure there was no lit sambuca still in the glass. Joey didn't check and there was, so when he pressed the glass over his nipple it stuck and melted it off.

Generally, the knobhead is harmless. A 'character'.

But we are in a time where knobheads seem to be the ones leading the way, and Joey is revelling in his new status. Cheerleader for action.

Alice is oblivious to all of this.

'Fairies keeping you entertained,' Paul said to her the other day.

'Eh?'

'Hope they are. Spending all your time off with them.'

And it is fair, Alice would agree. Of late, it is as if she is not fully in the room when she's there.

It would be an easy leap to guess why:

She has been furloughed from her job as a receptionist at The Lodge a local hotel and wedding venue.

But that's not it.

Something new is happening for her. Something she can't even explain to herself...

Ralph knows the route they are taking.

He is eager to be let off.

And once they are onto the track Alice lets him scamper away.

The ground rises sharply as they head out of the village towards the woods.

Weeks of blazing heat means the ground's hard. Dry. The grass starched from a lack of rain. Every step brings a crunch under the foot.

If Alice was to turn around she'd be able to point out every landmark, every house, the name of every occupant.

The most obvious starting point would be the closest building to her: the village hall. Well, *building* is a term that you would apply loosely in this instance. Implies solidity. The hall is far from that. For decades it has been in desperate need of renovation. The parish council has continually fought off the advances of developers to purchase the acre and a half of prime land that it occupies.

For years, the parish council have fundraised tirelessly: grants, donations, raffles, fetes, sponsored swims, runs, silences in Madeline Booths' case, all helped to chip slowly away at the monstrous target.

'Won't be round to see it done at this rate' was muttered on many occasions throughout the village.

'We'll turn the hall's field into a private car park. Charge visitors. Profits go to the redevelopment.'

This suggestion had been divisive within the parish committee and villagers:

'It's in the middle of the village – think of the extra traffic.'

'Short-term pain, long-term gain.'

The motion passed. And both sides of the coin were right: as word spread of a private car park that was the first spot for tourists to try, but in those two years it has provided such significant funds that by the end of the year the parish will have reached its funding goals.

But it is not the village hall and the lonely Audi A3 that sit within its makeshift carpark Alice would tell you about.

Alice would tell you about Bethany White, who is slowly walking to the churchyard with a handful of flowers.

Her husband, Mick, of fifty-eight years was buried there two weeks ago.

Today, like yesterday and the days before that, Bethany will sit by Mick's grave for nearly two hours. It is a routine that most of the village can now set their watch by. They don't disturb her. They let her talk to him.

'The black cap hasn't returned, be enjoying Spain too much. Left them those seeds you said they love, in case. I'll tempt him back.'

The plot next to Mick is where she will be buried when her times come – it's three years and twelve days away – she doesn't know that obviously – it's very peaceful, in her sleep.

Mick had spent the last year of his life in a hospice. The cancer was very aggressive.

The plan had been for him to spend his last months at home. It didn't work out how they hoped. So Bethany sat outside his window and watched him die.

His funeral was the hottest day of the year up to that point.

Some would say that was the key turning point in the village when tempers erupted over the visitors.

The village hall's temporary car park had been overrun by nine a.m., so people had started parking wherever they could.

Banksides. Over single yellows. Red Lion's customer car park. Drives. On the narrow lane towards the church.

Roads became barely passible for regular cars let alone for a hearse. A BMW had parked in such a way that the hearse couldn't take the narrow bend to the church. Paul, Joey, Will – Mick's son – and several others ended up trying to pick the car and moving it, in order to let Mick's body be laid to rest.

'Dump it in the stream – it's too heavy – tip it – made of lead this – put some welly in – take its wheels off.'

The hearse ended up having to reverse back through the lanes and in the end was two hours late for the scheduled service.

Later in the beer garden of The Red Lion, Will held court with many of the villagers.

'Only six allowed to say goodbye to my dad, but here, look around, whole world descends on us, like a pack of wolves. When that driver gets back.'

It was Bethany that broke up the chorus of approval:

'No. I want no fuss. Police will deal with it.'

'Mum –'

'No, William. Your dad would have found the funny side.'

And he would have done. That's the type of man he'd been. So, out of respect to Bethany, the villagers had not waited out for the driver to return, they left it to the police.

But Alice doesn't tell you any of this, because she doesn't turn, she keeps going. Following Ralph on his quest to inhale every blade of glass along the path.

Another gunshot echoes in the distance.

This time Alice does stop and look for the sound.

She wouldn't think it was coming from Harry's garden.

He is the nice accountant that hosts The Red Lion's quiz.

Normally it would be from the Scott Farm that the path she is walking on intersects.

Crows or rabbits or foxes the targets.

But it is Harry, and this time he hasn't missed.

From where Alice is stood, nobody in the world's eyesight is good enough to see the colour that Harry's face turns.

Di can see it though, as she is looking out from their kitchen window.

The noise hadn't surprised her. She'd seen the trigger being pulled. Watched the elation that ran through Harry as he realised that he'd hit it. She tracked him as he took the forty steps from the open tent to the grass by the strawberries. And then freezing. The complexion gained from the hours in the garden vanishing.

Harry was using Di's uncle's shotgun. A family heirloom. Not an air rifle.

He always buys his meat from the butcher's. Skinned, prepped. He doesn't fish or participate in any other pursuit where gutting and skinning is required, or you encounter death.

Di steps out into the back garden. Harry's still not moved. Di's the first to break the silence.

'The tent can be packed up now then.'

He's still staring at the rabbit.

'It's in pieces.'

'Well, what did you think would happen?'

Harry doesn't answer. He just looks at Di. And she him. And it's the first time they have done this in a long time.

Eventually Di says: 'Come inside, have a tea, I'll sort that out.'

Harry does.

—

'Beat you.'

Hannah Oates is sat on a tree stump. Her running gear is the only indication that she has just run two miles. No sweat. No red face. No aching limbs.

Hannah's always been a keen runner. Cross country for school and county. Part of a club at university before fizzling out in London. But since losing her job and returning to her family home three months ago, she's thrown herself back into the routine. Ten miles a day is nothing for her.

Alice does not bite and she can't hold Hannah's stare. Instead she keeps walking up the hill. Deeper into the woods. Hannah follows.

It is amongst these trees they spent most of their teenage years.

Stealing cans of cider from their parents' cupboards or bought by the older boys like Paul. Joints rolled and passed. Planning their futures which seemed as limitless as the sky above them.

It is here that Alice got pregnant. And her and Hannah's lives began to splinter into different orbits.

They move with ease up the path. Memories everywhere.

At the start of the year, if someone had told Hannah she would be back living with her parents in six months' time, she'd have said that someone was describing her nightmare. But as the weeks have passed by she's discovered something reassuring about being back here.

'Hannah is so authentic, so real. Say "*slow*" Han, go on.'

She got that at work, colleagues, who all sounded the same as each other, referencing her accent. It got to the point where she spoke less and less or, when she did, she diluted it, but here, now, she can hear her twang coming back. And it is comforting. It is her.

'Slow down', she calls out to Alice.

Alice doesn't, without looking back she says: 'Not got long.'

Hannah quickens her pace and pulls up alongside Alice.

'Going to look at me?'

Alice is still walking, staring dead straight ahead: 'Ralph??'

'He's fine, he's up there. Alice. Stop.'

There's a year's difference between them. Hannah a year older. They've been in and out of each other's lives since Hannah's parents moved into the village when she was three years old. The last four years though there has barely been any contact. Different lives. Different places.

'Look at me. Alice, it's just me.'

'It's not though, is it.'

Alice is looking at Hannah now. The woods are silent, you can almost hear her fingers trembling.

'We can talk about it, Al.'

'Think it's gone past that.'

When they kissed yesterday, it wasn't the act that shocked Alice, it was more the weight of several years being lifted. That finally something made sense. And this time when they do again it only cements the feeling.

A butterfly lands on a nearby wildflower, birds call from treetop to treetop, life is truly lived.

Ralph's barking.

They pull away and curse.

Not because Ralph's missing but because he's walking through the bushes with Ferret.

'That's a bit tasty.' Ferret's whistling as he saunters over, smirk the length of his face.

Hannah tells him very bluntly to leave. To stop being a creep.

And this, it just makes it worse, prick his interest even more.

'Creep? Bit rude. I'm just having a little morning stroll. Not the one getting all filthy in the woods.'

'It's not what it looks like.'

'Oh yeah, what's that? I know Paul likes tickling trout, didn't know you did too.'

Before Alice can say anything, Ralph's charged off up the hill, barking.

'Ralph!'

'Life lesson, keep things on a lead. I'll remind Paul.'

'Ferret, don't.'

'Please does go a long way in the world.'

'Please.'

'Better be after that dog of yours, know Paul would hate to lose that as well. I'm joking!'

And he's laughing as he heads off, cutting up to the brow of the hill, to the spot where Madeline swore she saw lights the night before.

Hannah speaks:

'He's stirring.'

'He's not.'

'And if he's not, is it a problem?'

'God's sake, Hannah. Paul.'

They don't say anything, neither of them need to acknowledge that Paul's a decent man. That becoming a dad at twenty-three had made him a better person than anyone ever thought possible. That it curbed all his youthful hot-headedness. Made him knuckle down and train up as an electrician. A job enables him to provide for his family, a family he cares for beyond words.

'What is this?' It's Hannah that asks the questions.

'I don't know.'

'Yes, you do.'

And Hannah's right, she does. But it's not something Alice was ready to talk about, or to be public and now...

'Ferret won't say anything. I'll make sure of it.'

And with that Hannah starts running. It's not long before she has caught Ferret up.

He is frozen. A gangly statue, stood in the middle of a little sheltered enclave, a secret spot that only those who grow up in the village would know. It's where fires are made and danced round. Where ghost stories are told, and first kisses shared. It's idyllic.

Normally.

Now though it looks like a rubbish truck has crashed into it, or a plane exploded in the sky above, spilling its guts.

Beer cans, bottles, little grey nitrous oxide cannisters are scattered everywhere. A foldable chair on its side, a tent broken in two, tubes of Pringles, food and wrappers, packets of half-filled sausages, tins of half-eaten beans, a bread loaf two slices left uneaten. And at its centre a disposable barbecue upended, its shape scorched into the soil.

And there is a smell.

Not just the spilt alcohol and the fat from the food...

It's shit.

Human.

Toilet paper squashed down on top creating several rancid molehills.

Ferret can barely speak. Just a noise.

A growl.

Hurt. Evolving into anger.

Then a word: 'Bastards'. Repeated over and over.

'Ferret, who did this?'

'Bastards.'

'Why, would...?' Hannah can't finish the question. It seems unfathomable. The destruction.

Ferret's taking photos on his phone.

'Bastards.'

Suddenly it makes sense as to why he is called Ferret. He is up on his tiptoes, sniffing, peering, his narrow body reaching up as high as possible, beady eyes scanning.

'That way.'

Ferret's quick, even in walking boots, his long limbs covering the ground with ease.

As they cut through the woods, Ferret's multitasking, checking, searching for signal on his phone.

'Who you calling?'

There's still a thought lingering in Hannah about what Ferret had interrupted and who he might be calling but when he answers it's clear that's a million miles from his mind.

'Turds were fresh.'

Suddenly Hannah realises: they're hunting.

'Bastards.'

They are out of the woods now. The sunlight dazzles them. The whole village before them. And that's when they see them. Four, five hundred metres away, three figures, weaving through the long grass. Snaking their way along the path towards the village hall and its car park in the distance.

It is no longer a jog, it's a full-on sprint. Ferret's mobile pings back into life. He's calling:

'Joey, you at top road? Need you at the hall. Pronto.'

–

As they walk through the long summer grass, Gee, Miller and Rads are oblivious to the events unfolding around them.

It had been a three-hour drive for them to get to the village.

The great outdoors.

They had made jokes about films like *Deliverance* and *Texas Chainsaw Massacre* on the way.

Gee had remembered going to the area as a kid with her mum. She remembered the space, the freedom, all that green, the hours spent laughing rolling down hills with her two siblings and then the journey back watching through the car window as the bright colours faded back to grey.

Recently she had read an online article about the best areas to go out exploring, but the specifics of the location, this village, no, they didn't know that's where they were going to end up. All they knew is that they had supplies, and a nineteen-pound pop-up tent and that they were going to party like the world was about to end.

Normally they would be out three times a week. Saturday was always the biggest night. Hit the pubs, a club, a curry if they hadn't got lucky. But for four months they'd just been indoors. No rituals. Stuck inside their shared flat, above the busy high street in the grey town that they lived in.

They had got lucky with a space in the hall car park. Arriving at that time of day when many were ending theirs. After popping a tenner in the parking metre, they had loaded up with their kit, jumped over the wall at the back of the hall and walked amidst the cows as they took the most direct route up into the woods.

The fresh air almost knocks them out.

It was luck that had lead them to the clearing in the woods.

Pop up tent did exactly as it was designed to do.

As the night drew in and the booze flowed their worries faded. Jokes came thick and fast and they gawped at the stars that shone on them and then next thing they knew was that gunshots woke them.

You don't hear them in the town they are from.

A sure way to clear groggy heads.

They take in the surroundings. There was nothing there they'd ever need again. Pointless really taking it with them. Lugging it all that way.

When they start heading back, there is no clarity about the route they took to get there.

'Too many trees. All looks the same.'

And so they go back and forth, lost in circles, till finally they reach the edge of the woods.

–

Joey's not by himself when he gets Ferret's call.

Tommy Scott has just pulled up in his tractor alongside him, ready to deposit another haybale in the middle of the road.

The summer for Tommy has been spent closing gates where cows had wandered out from. Of shooing walkers off his land that has been freshly seeded as they traipse through it.

'THERE'S A PATH!'

He'd point at it. Occasionally he'd get a sorry but mostly it was shrugs and the middle finger that he'd get back.

The first two cars that arrived had quickly turned back when the two strapping locals declared the village was closed.

But right now, there is a Mondeo full of a family with thick city accents beeping their horn at them.

'Public road!'

'Not today.'

'We've driven nearly hundred miles to get here.'

'And you can drive back there. We don't want you.'

The language escalates quickly. Threats to call the police.

'Phone them, go on, see how long it takes, be a good three hours, minimum, before they do.'

Thankfully for the passengers in the Mondeo, Joey and Tommy hadn't yet seen the photos of the campsite that Ferret has sent to the village community action WhatsApp group, otherwise it might have been more than words and gestures and stares that they got, before they raced away in fear.

–

Phones are pinging throughout the village.

Once Ferret's photos were unleashed the response in the WhatsApp group is like a tidal wave of anger.

Clothes are hastily thrown on.

Suntan lotion forgotten.

Teas left half-drunk.

Front doors being thrown open in unison and a march through the village begins.

–

Alice and Paul had recently left the village WhatsApp group. It was like having a little chaffinch in the room. Every other second. Ting, ting, ting. What had originally started with the aim of fostering a sense of community, now felt like the group's sole aim was to generate rage and suspicion.

'Reads like a bloody lynch mob,' Paul would sigh.

So when Alice, out of breath from running back from the woods, looks in through the kitchen window all she sees is domestic bliss.

It's breakfast time.

Cereal in bowls.

TV playing in the background.

'We're up early. Ralph looks grateful.' Paul says between sips of tea.

Alice nods, her home still normal. Clearly Hannah got to Ferret.

'Go far?'

'Just to the top.'

Paul's phone's ringing. 'What now?'

'Everything okay?'

'Ferret.'

'Ignore it.'

'Only keep ringing – bet he's locked himself out again, something stupid.'

'Muuuuum, can Sally come and play today?'

Alice isn't really listening when she responds to Carly.

'…In the garden – if her mum says so.'

She's listening, watching Paul's reactions to the phone call.

'What? Jesus.'

He hangs up. Pushes the chair away. Domestic bliss broken.

'Paul?'

'There's some hoo-ha, better go, try and put the fire out.'

And maybe it is the relief that stops Alice from instantly saying she'll come with him but by the time she says it, it is too late, Paul's gone.

'Carly, put a film on, I'll be five minutes, the remote's…'

Carly shrugs: 'I *know* where the remote is'.

–

Hannah and Ferret are covering the ground quickly. It is touch and go if they will have caught up with the three figures before they arrive in the car park.

As they climb over the wall into the hall car park, Gee, Millar and Rads are beginning to clock that they are being pursued.

'Oi!' It's Ferret calling them out.

They don't stop. Millar presses the car-key button. The lights of his A3 flashing. Unlocked.

'OI!' Ferret again, as he climbs over the wall into the hall car park.

The car doors are open, but none have stepped in yet.

'Not going anywhere.'

Ferret can see the colour of Rads's eyes when he turns. There is no fear. They are crystal clear.

'WHAT?'

Rads's aggression is enough to make Ferret pause for a second.

Rads was a good amateur boxer. Next to him, Millar is not as skilled, lost more fights than he has won, what he makes up for in skill though is toughness and a love of the confrontation. Never afraid to get hit to do some damage back. Gee understands this language too and she knows that she would have no problem battering the girl that has just arrived next to the skinny man.

It is silent for a moment. Five people, eyes locked.

Ferret has his phone held out, righteous anger driving him, oblivious to the numerical disadvantage:

'Dirty bastards that did this.'

'No, we didn't.'

The denial comes quick from Gee. It's indignant. And angry. And quickly all five become embroiled in a slinging match of words:

'Think it's alright to do that do you??!!'

'WASN'T US!'

'Liars!'

'Can't prove it.'

'Would you like if I shat on your doorstep? Would you?'

'IT'S IN THE WOODS NOT YOUR DOORSTEP.'

'DON'T RECORD ME.'

Millar has stepped towards Ferret who has started to record them on his phone.

'GOING ON YOUTUBE.'

'I'll smash that right out of your hands.'

Rads and Gee are joining Millar as he steps towards Ferret and Hannah.

'Don't come closer!' It's Hannah who is speaking, her heart racing.

'OR WHAT?'

The question hangs in the air.

Then suddenly thump.

A haybale.

Its Tommy Scott.

His tractor dropping it, blocking any exit for a car.

Joey's striding towards the group.

'That them?'

'Yeah, threatening us,' Ferret nods.

'That right?'.

'No'. It's Millar that says that. Aware the atmosphere is changing, that they are becoming trapped, not just by the haybale but the arrival of more villagers behind Joey, many of them still in dressing gowns, armed with mobile phones recording every word.

'Dirty pigs.'

'Wasn't us.'

'Come here and do that.'

'No respect for the world.'

'We didn't do it.'

'Why do you think that's appropriate?'

'Awful, just awful.'

'They can't even own it.'

'Who brought you up?'

'People like you, ruining this world!'

Gee's got her phone out and is recording those recording herself – it's a modern shield.

'Get that off her!' – it's Joey leading the pack.

And there's many people willing to take it.

'Touch me and I'll sue you'

'Fat chance, you will.'

'Grab it!'

It's Paul's voice that cuts through: 'What you all doing?'

'Look at what they did, dirty bastards.' Ferret's got his phone in front of Paul, showing him the carnage.

'They did that? Well call the police then.'

'Take them all day, and then they'll do what?'

'Whatever they can do, Joey, that's what.'

'Last time, they said, deal with it yourselves.'

The officer had actually said: 'We're stretched, asking for your help in these times', clumsy perhaps, the word 'help' left so open to interpretation.

Gee, Millar and Rads have gone quiet. Each aware that Paul is potentially offering them a route out.

But Paul is clearly in the minority. The rest of the villagers are no longer silent, they are back hunting for blood.

'We're not calling police.' Will White snarls, his fist clenching

– finally he has found targets for all the anger he has had stored since his dad's funeral.

Alice is out of breath when she arrives.

She can hear Paul acting the peacemaker, the three strenuously denying it, villagers becoming more and more angry.

And it is annoying Joey and Ferret and many of the others how righteous Paul is being:

'We're not the law.'

Ferret, well everyone, knows that deep down Paul has got a mean streak. The streak he had as a kid that gave him a bad name, that he's spent years doing his best to forget, but that still lingers. It just needs to be poked and prodded in order to be unleashed. And it is easy for Ferret. He's got a secret that will light the fuse:

'Being all mardy, because your missus loves a bit of quim?'

Paul looks at Alice, more confused than shocked: what is he on about?

'This pigsty isn't the only thing I saw up in them woods: eating each other's face they were.'

Rumours are what the village lives on, but this was something none had seen coming.

Paul knows it is true, just by the look on Alice's face.

He's silent taking in everyone.

Finally, he states to the three outsiders:

'You're going to fix it.'

–

There are at least twenty cameras filming Gee, Millar and Rads as they traipse back up to the woods.

The heat now beating down on them, sweat dripping and oozing from every pore.

Each step they are being asked the same questions:

'How, why, what's your problem, do that outside your own home, it's disgusting, shame on you.'

They are not denying it any more, there is no real justification coming back, it's more the surprise that people care so much that strikes them. And they just nod. The sooner it is done the sooner they get through it.

Maybe they look at it differently now that they are walking into the mess: the chaos, the filth.

'Get on with it then', Paul tells them.

They start with the cans and bottles, the furniture.

Doesn't take them long.

That's what amuses many of the people pointing the camera at them.

It was so easy. Popped straight into the plastic bags they had left scattered amidst the trees.

'Not hard is it.'

The food's trickier. Messier. Sausages split, meat oozing out.

'Dirty scrubbers,' Joey's muttering.

And for a moment hearing that Rads is back at school. The twelve-year old been mocked for coming in in a dirty uniform again.

'And all them beans.' Paul's pointing at them.

'Got no bags left.' Millar's quiet when he says that.

'Got pockets, got your rucksack, leave nothing behind.'

There are sniggers when Rads puts beans into his shorts pocket.

'Forgetting something?'

Gee, Millar and Rads take in the surroundings. The food, the cans, the barbecue, the tent and chair all bagged or ready to be carried away. All that remains are five mounds of toilet paper.

'Really?'

'Course, really.'

They take in the villagers, circled round them. Some no longer meeting their eyes.

'Which one were yours?' It's Rads that asks Gee.

'I don't remember.'

'We've got no bags.'

'Bury it then', Paul tells them.

'Bury it?'

'Yeah, dig a hole'.

'What with?'

'Sticks. Hands.'

Hannah's been silent this whole time. It's felt like eyes have been as much on her as they are on the group of outsiders, but she can't stay quiet any longer: 'Someone must have dog bags for them.'

'No, they don't,' Paul says, before anyone volunteers. And no one steps forward. Hannah looks to Alice, she's looking at the floor. Just like some of the others, some who have stopped recording. Phones now back in their pockets. Shuffling awkwardly in dressing gowns.

They dig with sticks and hands.

The ground's hard, so it takes longer than many expected.

Millar brushes flies away from one of the mounds. He's about to use two sticks as a shovel.

'Here.' Tommy Scott throws some dog bags towards him, 'Use them'.

'Get on with it,' Paul tells them.

The trees sway in the wind, the sun breaks through into the clearing.

With packed bags they trudge back.

In the car park it feels like the whole village watches them pile their possessions into the boot.

'We're going to follow you, make sure you don't just tip as soon as you're round the corner,' Paul tells them.

'They won't do it again, will you.' Its Harry now that takes over as the village's calm reference point.

And they nod. And get in the car, and with the haybale now moved drive off and out of the village.

There's no music playing, no radio, no words shared as they drive through the lanes.

After four miles Millar pulls into a passing point. He gets out. The birds the only sound for miles. Gee and Rads watch Millar from inside the car. They watch his breathing becoming more and more out of control. They had forgotten he had asthma. Rads rummages in the car. Under the seat he eventually finds a plastic bag.

'Here.' Millar takes deep breaths.

When he retires in thirty-six years, a colleague asks Rads why he decided to become a nurse. He won't remember it's this moment, years of service jading him, in fact he barely remembers Millar and Gee so part of a life he long left behind. But it is this moment, the way Millar listens to him as he calms, as he realises the euphoria of healing.

The three of them sit by the verge.

The world around them so calm, so peaceful.

They know what is ahead of them when they get home.

And then they think about what is ahead for those they just left in the village.

Millar opens the boot. Gee and Rads join him.

They take every item they had packed back up and throw it onto the verge, into the hedges –

'AHHHHHHH!!!!!'

Eventually their voices give in.

They then drive back to their flat above a shop with a view of more of the same.

—

Today if you looked round the village you'd still find tensions.

You'd still find villagers patrolling, that the WhatsApp group is a hive of paranoid activity.

You'd discover that Paul begged Alice to stay, that she has but the end is inevitable.

You'd discover that when it comes Alice's new beginnings won't involve Hannah, as she's gone back to London, a place where she can be invisible, where nobody knows her business.

You'd know that Joey broke his foot jumping out of a moving car.

You'd know that Harry and Di now sleep in the same bed and the rabbits have found another crop to attack.

You'd know that Will loaded a video of the incident up on YouTube, that it went viral, and that Millar was spotted by his employer and sacked, you wouldn't know though that for the next two years he struggles to pick up work, and that he and Gee have a baby together in a smaller flat in a greyer part of town. A baby that will grow into a man who becomes a soldier, who loses his leg in a field thousands of miles from the town he was desperate to escape from.

You'd know that when the new hall opens in seven years' time, many villagers will never accept that it's strangers, people that will never step inside that are just as responsible for its creation as those that live within the village.

—

Now think back to that map.

This took place within two tiny squares.

A two-kilometre squared area.

There are over two hundred thousand square miles in Great Britain.

This story is not unique.

It may not be heard regularly, on major news channel but it plays out multiple times in multiple places.

So how do we move forward together?

How do we all learn from it?

Because this is not something that is going away, certainly not in the short term.

I asked you to close your eyes before, now though I'm going to ask you to do the opposite.

Look around, who do we think this belongs to?

The sky? The trees? The views? The sounds? The smells?

Those who live here? Those who visit? Those who have never been given a chance to understand it? Those who love it?

Who?

What right does anyone have to this? To something that was here before us and will be here for years after we've gone?

…

The End.

A Nick Hern Book

The Wife of Cyncoed and *Idyll* first published in Great Britain as a paperback original in 2024 by Nick Hern Books Limited, The Glasshouse, 49a Goldhawk Road, London W12 8QP, in association with the Sherman Theatre, Cardiff

The Wife of Cyncoed copyright © 2024 Matt Hartley
Idyll copyright © 2024 Matt Hartley

Matt Hartley has asserted his right to be identified as the author of these works

Cover photography by Burning Red
Back cover image by Pentabus Theatre via iStock

Designed and typeset by Nick Hern Books, London
Printed in Great Britain by Mimeo Ltd, Huntingdon, Cambridgeshire PE29 6XX

A CIP catalogue record for this book is available from the British Library

ISBN 978 1 83904 319 2

CAUTION All rights whatsoever in these plays are strictly reserved. Requests to reproduce the texts in whole or in part should be addressed to the publisher.

Amateur Performing Rights Applications for performance, including readings and excerpts, by amateurs in the English language should be addressed to the Performing Rights Manager, Nick Hern Books, The Glasshouse, 49a Goldhawk Road, London W12 8QP, *tel* +44 (0)20 8749 4953, *email* rights@nickhernbooks.co.uk, except as follows:

Australia: ORiGiN Theatrical, *tel* +61 (2) 8514 5201,
email enquiries@originmusic.com.au, *web* www.origintheatrical.com.au

New Zealand: Play Bureau, 20 Rua Street, Mangapapa, Gisborne 4010,
tel +64 21 258 3998, *email* info@playbureau.com

United States of America and Canada: United Agents, see details below

Professional Performing Rights Applications for performance by professionals in any medium and in any language throughout the world should be addressed to United Agents, 12–26 Lexington St, London W1F 0LE, *tel* +44 (0)20 3214 0800, *fax* +44 (0)20 3214 0801, *email* info@unitedagents.co.uk

No performance of any kind may be given unless a licence has been obtained. Applications should be made before rehearsals begin. Publication of these plays does not necessarily indicate their availability for amateur performance.

www.nickhernbooks.co.uk/environmental-policy

www.nickhernbooks.co.uk

facebook.com/nickhernbooks

twitter.com/nickhernbooks